ATLANTA'S
OLYMPIC RESURGENCE

D1300548

ATLANTA'S
OLYMPIC RESURGENCE

How the 1996 Games Revived a Struggling City

MICHAEL DOBBINS, LEON S. EPLAN & RANDAL ROARK

Foreword by Clara Hayley Axam

THE
History
PRESS

Published by The History Press
Charleston, SC
www.historypress.com

Back cover, inset: Olympic flag. *Wikimedia Commons*; Dr. Edwin P Ewing Jr., Centers for Disease Control and Prevention.

First published 2021

Manufactured in the United States

ISBN 9781467147248

Library of Congress Control Number: 2021931153

CONTENTS

FOREWORD

I was skeptical from the beginning—not at all sure if Atlanta was serious about embracing Mayor Maynard Jackson's approach to preparing the city for the 1996 Games: twin peaks, one that focused on preparing venues and delivering facilities to house the Games and another that focused on leaving a legacy that would help reboot a city experiencing population decline, disinvestment and increasing inequities. For weeks, the inner-city neighborhoods had been in an uproar over the disruption they anticipated from construction of facilities followed by the throngs of visitors who would invade their neighborhoods to enter those facilities and attend the Games.

My first few months as president of the Corporation for Olympic Development in Atlanta (CODA)—created by Mayor Jackson to manage the legacy agenda—did little to quell my skepticism. Encouraged by Mayor Jackson and Mayor Andrew Young, I set in motion my plan to speak to public, private, nonprofit and community leadership about their willingness to embrace a "twin peaks agenda." And for months, I felt more like a ping pong ball tossed between the sectors than the president of an organization that hoped to leave a legacy for the city we all claimed to love.

In all honesty, I'm not sure when it started to occur to the leadership of our city that it would take the "collective leadership" of the public, private and nonprofit sectors to succeed with either peak. The Atlanta Games were to be privately funded. Atlanta would have to make use of every resource and asset—many of which were public. Policy decisions were required to support the preparations on city streets *and* private property. Foundation dollars were needed to sweeten the pot, fill in the gaps and cover the shortfalls if the city was to deliver the Games debt-free as promised. And then there were the community voices that insisted that their interest in a better quality of life would not be crushed in the name of "economic progress," *again*.

Perhaps the reality that neither public nor private sector could be successful alone occurred as the city began to face the monumental task of delivering on the promises in the city's successful bid for the Games. Or perhaps it occurred in some of the many robust discussions where the city wrestled with its history of segregation, its identity and what it meant to leave an Olympic legacy. Hindsight has a way of romanticizing history—and sometimes revising it. I bear witness that the revelation of the new reality did not come easy or without tensions. But at some point, the leadership of Atlanta realized that a successful 1996 Games would require a public/private sector partnership like none before and possibly none since.

You, perhaps, will find the answer in the pages of this book. I am sure it is here in the story as told by Leon Eplan, who, as Commissioner of Planning for the City of Atlanta, became the main author of the city's 1996 Games' plan; Randal Roark, then professor of architecture and planning at the prestigious Georgia Institute of Technology who became the full-time visionary director of planning for CODA; and Michael Dobbins, the city's post-Games commissioner of planning who had the opportunity to build on the impact of the Olympic Games' wake and encourage subsequent development.

The authors present the fascinating story of how Atlanta, in preparing for the 1996 Games, serendipitously found itself forging a new partnership—planning not just for the Games, but for the city's future with intentionality, putting Atlanta on the road to realizing its dream of being known as a world-class city.

—Clara Hayley Axam, president of CODA

PREFACE

The transformative myth of the phoenix, a bird that rises again and again from the ashes of destruction, has long been the symbol of the city of Atlanta. It was adopted in 1887 as the symbol of the city, proclaiming the "new South" arising from the ash heap of the destruction of the Civil War in 1864. The phoenix has continued to represent the city's struggle to rise, to reach a place among the great cities of the world. Nowhere in Atlanta's recent history has this story been more prominent than in the city's effort to overcome the decline of population, disinvestment and demolition in its core leading up to the Olympics. The city was struggling to overcome the shroud of its Jim Crow past through mounting struggles against racism and rising assertion of civil rights underway since the 1960s.

Then, ironically, in this continuing population decline, the city won the bid to host the Centennial Olympic Games for 1996. Credit is due to the heroic efforts of several business leaders, Mayor Andy Young and other public officials. The presence of a few good-quality sports venues and a blossoming convention industry further strengthened the case. At this improbable confluence, the newly elected mayor of the city, Maynard Jackson Jr., a son of Atlanta's storied civil rights generation, seized the moment to put forth a dual agenda, which he termed the "Twin Peaks of Mount Olympics": the Games, yes, but the city too. He acted to stage a successful and memorable Olympic Games while harnessing and leveraging its energy to address the problems facing the city. His goal

Atlanta from the Ashes Phoenix Monument, Woodruff Park. *Dixi Carrillo.*

was to transform Atlanta's urban legacy. This book is the story of this improbable moment in this improbable city.

As this book nears publication in the spring of 2021, it is now a quarter of a century since the 1996 Olympic Games took place. With the passage of time and the advantage of hindsight and data, we see how that period in Atlanta history catalyzed a sea change in its transformation. Atlanta is now the center of a robust multicultural urban region, nearing six million people. That twenty-five-year progression marked cautious but growing collaborations between governments, the private sector and communities. We posit that the impact of the changes catalyzed by the Olympic Games initiative and the legacy projects that followed played a pivotal role in these demographic shifts. The transforming regional settlement patterns were decisive in determining the outcome of the 2020 election: a Democratic president and two Democratic senators.

The book also tells two other important stories. The first considers the Atlanta Games in the context of the modern Olympic movement. From our 2021 vantage point, we recognize the significance of our story against the backdrop of the Olympic movement. Borne of white European colonial mentality 125 years ago, now facing international cultural shifts and with the Tokyo Games imperiled by the pandemic, the future of the movement is problematic. Yet the Games still represent the only peaceful gathering of all the world's nations.

The Atlanta Olympics was truly an anomaly compared to other cities that have hosted the event. Atlanta was the smallest of these cities, and its Games were the least expensive—incurring no municipal debt—and the most privately financed since Los Angeles in 1984.

Yet Atlanta perhaps represents a way forward to leverage the potential of the Olympics to address the kinds of problems facing the city at the time, based on Mayor Jackson's "twin peaks" agenda. Thus, almost unwittingly, Atlanta may have created a model useful for future Olympics cities for how to stage a low impact but high yield event, with a legacy reaching far beyond the Games themselves. The 2012 London Olympics, for example, committed to a process more socially oriented, more transparent, and more integrative of workforce priorities in its economic model than other cities. We hope that our Atlanta Olympics story, which reflects a public sector perspective, may be useful to future host cities in their efforts to capture benefits and narrow the gap between what is often promised but rarely realized.

While not focused on the Olympic movement itself, our book shows that the Atlanta Games were something of an anomaly in this highly charged mega event environment.

The second story demonstrates the power of planning and collaboration of myriad public, private, nonprofit and community entities to achieve long-lasting goals. The short time frame and pressure-cooked environment of the staging of an Olympic Games demanded that all come together to meet the absolute deadline. It focuses on how the city built on the forced partnerships that delivered the Olympics in order to change public development policy, planning practice and financing to better guide continuing collaborations. It then describes how these new arrangements succeeded, or not, in delivering a number of projects whose roots trace to their beginnings in the Olympics moment.

ABOUT THE AUTHORS

We tell this story as lifelong practitioners and teachers of the planning skills necessary to undertake our successive missions during this time. We acted as principals in the city government's planning, design and implementation work to prepare, deliver and follow up on the Olympic opportunity. Thus, we write as chroniclers, diarists or memoirists, recollecting our experiences and reflecting on these most significant portions of our working lives. We recount firsthand history as active participants over that period, here defined as the fifteen-year period from 1990, the announcement of Atlanta's winning the bid, into the early 2000s. At the center of our story, our positions were:

- Leon Eplan, Atlanta's commissioner of planning and development in the Olympic run-up period, who created the city's Olympic Development Program;
- Randal Roark, director of planning and development for the Corporation for Olympic Development in Atlanta, the implementing agency for the city's Olympic plan;
- Michael Dobbins, the city's commissioner of planning, development and neighborhood conservation from the Games going forward into the early 2000s.

We have collaborated on all facets of the book, but each of us has taken primary responsibility for coordination, oversight and editing for those portions of the story with which he was most directly involved. In chapters 1 and 2, Leon sets the city's pre-Olympic stage and explains how the city got the Games. He also enumerates how, working for Mayor Jackson, he prepared the city's Olympic Development Plan. That work included setting up the Corporation for Olympic Development in Atlanta (CODA) as the city's implementation agency. In chapter 3, Randy, as director of design and development for CODA, recounts the full CODA story—its beginnings, its tasks, its resources, its challenges and its accomplishments—over three years of intense and game-changing activity. In chapter 4, he documents the sources and uses of Olympic funding and compares them with other Olympic cities in the same time frame. Finally, in chapters 5 and 6, working for Mayor Bill Campbell, Mike picks up from these Olympic development generators and carries the book through the city's policy and planning initiatives aimed toward forging ongoing neighborhood and developer collaborations to take advantage of the Olympics catalyst.

The book sets the broader historical context for the complete story. We believe that our documentation of the Atlanta experience will significantly expand the range of inquiry for historians and others interested in digging more deeply into the Olympics generally, the Atlanta games, Atlanta's history and the machinery of Atlanta governance.

Introduction

KNOWING ATLANTA

A Rocky Century

As backdrop for our book, we offer a picture of Atlanta as it was approaching the international center stage as the host city of the Olympic Games. Prior to the 1992 Barcelona Games, leaders in the International Olympic Committee (IOC) in Lausanne, Switzerland, began to discuss using the 1996 Games to commemorate the centennial year of the beginning of the modern Games. Only a few Atlanta residents, and certainly none with the IOC, would have realized that Atlanta would also be commemorating a centennial year of its own. Two of the city's most notable historic moments would be bracketed by events set apart by almost 100 years: the Cotton States and International Exposition in 1895 and then 101 years later the 1996 Games. Throughout that long duration, Atlanta experienced many changes, some uplifting and rewarding, full of memorable and challenging years. Others would be difficult and upending, testing the ability of citizens to withstand several quite turbulent years, with wide swings in the economy and breakdowns in the social cohesion. These times tested the city's civic leadership and its capability to manage the constant changes, some placid and others disruptive. Now the city was facing the huge demands the Olympics would bring.

Atlanta's century began with the opening of the gates to the Cotton States Exposition on September 18, 1895. The exposition brought Atlanta together with Georgia and five other southeastern states to attract trade from the

Five Points Monument at historic five points intersection. *Neil Dent; artist George Beasley.*

Five Points Water Tower, 1857. *Atlanta History Center.*

nation's northern industrial and emerging midwestern areas, particularly to market cotton, the area's chief agricultural product. President Grover Cleveland arrived to give the inaugural address. Atlanta was then a city of 86,000 residents, modest in size, but clearly anxious to grow. More people were moving in and launching new projects of a scale previously unseen. Apart from its much older rival, New Orleans, the city had become the largest urban place within the relatively undeveloped American Southeast. All in all, when the exposition closed three months later, it had attracted almost 800,000 visitors. The exposition's sponsor felt that the response from throughout the nation was quite favorable.

For Atlanta, however, a second goal for the event mattered even more. The city wanted to show itself to the nation as a revitalized community and dispel any lingering images of the town that only thirty years earlier had been almost totally destroyed by fire, following one of the last great battles of the American Civil War. Now, a strong and emerging economy replaced its war-torn past, and the city had become the leader of a new South. Buildings at the exposition demonstrated the region's modern technologies in agriculture, manufacturing and transportation. And, unusual for the time, exhibits showed advancements made by women and Black people, albeit through the paternalist lens of an all-white male power structure.

From this high, only eleven years later, in 1906, Atlanta squandered that positive status when it encountered a brief, but debilitating, race riot. More a massacre than a riot, white Atlantans were rebelling against the gains Black citizens had been achieving during Reconstruction. Inflammatory, fake, anti-Black news underpinned the gubernatorial campaigns of Clark Howard, editor of the *Atlanta Constitution* and Hoke Smith, publisher of the *Atlanta Journal*. A white mob went on a rampage, killing more than two dozen Black residents, wounding many more and destroying many places of emerging Black business. Newspapers across the country showed the city in another light, one different and unfavorable to the progressive image white city leaders had been seeking to communicate.

More damaging, the circumstances around that event were not soon to be altered. The growing expectation Black people had for a better life was reversed by more rigid segregation ordinances, mirroring the imposition of Jim Crow laws throughout the South. These harshly oppressive times amassed fortunes for many of the city's white elites by the exploitation of so-called convict labor. Across the South, thousands of innocent Black citizens, mostly men, were regularly rounded up, convicted on trumped-up charges and literally sold to white captains of industry and agriculture.

Perhaps ugliest among these in Atlanta, hundreds so condemned were indentured to the Chattahoochee Brick Company, where brutal work conditions sent untold numbers of Black men and several women to their deaths. (For a thorough documentation of this practice and its horrors, see Douglas Blackmon's *Slavery by Another Name*.) In many industries, the labor force built by the practice greatly enriched their owners by undercutting the mostly white and "free" labor force. From that nadir, it would take more than fifty years for permanent change in Atlanta's racial relationships to begin to emerge as Black Atlantans began to tackle issues of equity and justice.

With the advent of the twentieth century, the nation became engaged in two world wars. In both, Atlanta assumed important military, industrial and transportation roles. Especially during World War II, tens of thousands of military and civilian personnel descended on the city, drawn by the interchange of four rail lines and several highway junctions. Wartime products arrived, were assembled and then shipped out. Warehouses were constructed to store military supplies, and commercial enterprises quickly began operations. Military and civilian housing was added to underpin a rapidly growing population.

Then, rather abruptly, the war ended, and much of the city's frenetic life generated by the conflict, almost to the point of turmoil, subsided. Longtime white residents anxiously welcomed a return to their more accustomed peacetime mode. Black residents hoped that moves toward leveling the playing field they had experienced in the military would carry over to civilian life.

The forces of change pushed Atlanta beyond its prewar conditions. After the armistice, the huge military operations and related buildup were disassembled, and the accompanying tumult that had considerably enlarged both private and city functions vanished. Many of the people drawn to the city by the wartime activities also left. But some remained. Scores of individuals and families who had established families decided to put down permanent roots. Owners of new commercial enterprises launched during the war years chose not to abandon their investments but, instead, settled down. Growth was now occurring in almost every sector of the city and then spilled out into the entire region. In 1946, only months following the end of the conflict, plans were quickly approved and construction began on a huge north–south, six-lane highway through the heart of the city. Reflecting this ferment, the population of both the city and region grew by 10 percent from 1940 levels.

Paralleling the growing white population, the city also began to attract a burgeoning Black population who began settling into the established culture of Black life and leadership, perhaps best reflected in the community of businesses and residents centered on and around Auburn Avenue—from Peachtree Street downtown east to the Old Fourth Ward. (Gary Pomerantz's *Where Peachtree Meets Sweet Auburn* documents these trajectories through the history and relationships of two of the city's most prominent Black and white families, those of John Wesley Dobbs and Ivan Allen.)

Initially, Atlanta continued to maintain the governmental and social structures that had been in place for most of its history. With only occasional deviations, the principal political powers, economic entities, civic organizations and private institutions remained largely as they had been, drawing their leadership exclusively from the mostly male, white and upper-income classes. William B. Hartsfield, who served as mayor, with the exception of one year, for twenty-four years, provided continuity stretching from the Depression and war years through the postwar period.

More recent arrivals, however, introduced greater diversity, different tastes and attitudes, wider religious and political choices and increased involvement in civic affairs. There were three factors that especially affected the changes taking place in Atlanta: race relations, demographics and governance.

Race Relations

Moving into the 1960s, every aspect of life in Atlanta remained separated by race—theaters, restaurants, jails, buses, drinking fountains, toilets, sports activities, schools, libraries, sports teams, voting and permits for assembly. Dual public systems enforced the separation. Then, in 1958, in a city some regarded as being comparatively moderate in matters concerning racial oppression, Atlanta swore in eight officers as the city's first policemen of color. There were restrictions on their assignments. For example, they could not drive patrol cars or patrol white neighborhoods, wear uniforms to or from work or arrest white people. Their assignment was to patrol Black neighborhoods and commercial districts. Black residents and business owners and supportive white residents and business owners accepted them. Their employment as sworn police officers was considered a small advance.

Despite the optimism that accompanied this small advance, many incidents of struggle and tension between the Black and white races continued to punctuate the years throughout the 1950s. Most grew from personal antagonisms and challenges to the impositions of Jim Crow conventions and restrictions of behavior. Seeking change, neatly dressed students from Morehouse and other nearby African American colleges began testing the extent of laws governing segregation. They entered retail stores, sat down at luncheon counters and ordered coffee. When refused service, they would remain, quietly, sometimes for hours. Finally, service would be closed to everyone. At times, students were arrested and taken to jail. Then, usually within hours, someone would come by, pay a fine and secure their release. Meanwhile, respectful but strained meetings were being held behind closed doors between white city official and business owners and Black leaders and business owners, all seeking ways to deal with hostilities and inequities. But little progress was made in bridging the differences.

Simultaneously, something else, less noticeable, was also occurring. Between 1950 and 1970, the size of the Black population gradually expanded, doubling from 121,000 to over 250,000 persons. Land in the city's crowded central area, which Jim Crow–era zoning laws consigned as mostly Black neighborhoods, became too dense to absorb further development. Limited in places to live, encouraged by a civil rights movement seeking change and enabled by federal civil rights legislative advances, Black families began to seek housing more broadly in the city. Sales to Black families began in neighborhoods adjacent to those typically occupied by Black residents, triggering white anger, resulting in mounting hostility and, in the worst cases, marked by the bombing of some houses. Despite these challenges, in a relatively short span of three to five years, the racial makeup in several neighborhoods changed from mostly white to mostly Black. By 1970, the combination of Black population growth and the momentum engendered by civil rights–induced integration had catalyzed major change for the city. Atlanta became the first large southern municipality with a majority Black population.

Even before Hartsfield stepped down as the city's mayor in 1960, decisions were being made far beyond the city and region that, in time, would permanently alter local area functions and relationships. Most important was the decision of the Supreme Court in *Brown v. Board of Education* in 1954, declaring that segregation of students by race in public schools was unconstitutional. This decision brought universal white resistance throughout the South and a call for total resistance. State legislatures adopted proposals to privatize the public school systems, eventually found to be illegal and financially untenable.

Later in the 1960s, additional congressional legislation outlawed discrimination in public accommodations and in voting. Federal agencies promptly followed up on this legislation with guidelines spelling out mandates for compliance as a condition for cities to receive federal monies. Access to funds related to urban housing, parks, schools, roads and other public activities were affected. The national economy was expanding, and local governments were eager to apply for these monies. Federal monies were needed to address growing demands for new and upgraded public facilities. Suburban areas were experiencing strong growth, and core cities were losing white population. While this confluence of events and shifts challenged the existing status quo, the adopted solution to use federal and local funds to underwrite new development, ostensibly without regard to color, in fact exacerbated segregation, at best doing little to bridge the racial divide.

Nevertheless, Atlanta was slowly embracing integration In August 1961, seven years following the court's ruling on public school segregation, nine Black children were the first to enroll in four formerly all-white city high schools. A large crowd, primarily composed of police, parents, reporters, politicians and neighborhood citizens, gathered to observe the event. The event was peaceful, unlike the troubled resistance that had occurred in other southern cities. In a press conference that day, President John Kennedy commended city leaders for organizing integration "with dignity and without incident" and urged other school systems to "look closely at what Atlanta has done." That same year, most stores in the Downtown, after years of tense negotiation with leaders in the Black community, integrated.

Early in the 1960s, Dr. Martin Luther King Jr., the leader of the country's civil rights movement, opened the offices of the Southern Christian Leadership Conference in Downtown Atlanta, making Atlanta the national center in the civil rights movement. In the quest for achieving racial equality, one of his missions as president of that organization was to coordinate a mass movement, including Black Protestant churches and community and workers' organizations. Traveling throughout large cities and small towns, his was the strong and leading voice in challenging laws and traditions underpinning segregation, in advocating nonviolent resistance to discrimination and unfair practices and, whenever possible, in negotiating a possible settlement in racial conflicts.

With Ivan Allen becoming mayor in 1960, separation of Black and white people in public places soon ended. Signs dividing restrooms by race and seating in public gathering places, including cafeterias, were removed. Those seeking public services were thereafter to be addressed as Mr. or Mrs. and treated equally regardless of their race. All court proceedings were to remove any indication of racial intolerance. The effort of Atlanta leadership in the 1960s to chip away at the vestiges of racism was taking place in few other southern cities. Many years would pass before national laws and judicial pronouncements calling for authentic integration were issued, and much more work would be required for integration to be not merely tolerated but accepted as the norm—a quest still resisted by many white citizens and organizations in not only the South, but elsewhere throughout the country as well. In Atlanta, it was a start.

Demographic Shifts

Leading up to the Olympics

It was during the peacetime years following World War II that an era of permanent change began. Initially, Atlanta continued to maintain the governmental and social structures that had been in place for most of its history. With only occasional deviations, the principal political powers, economic entities, civic organizations and private institutions remained largely as they had been, drawing their leadership exclusively from the white middle- and upper-income classes. Continuity was provided by William B. Hartsfield, who served, with the exception of one year, as mayor for twenty-four years, stretching from the Depression and the war years through the postwar period.

By the end of the 1950s, growth in both the city and the region took significantly different courses, the trends moving in opposite directions. The city was rapidly losing population, while considerable growth was taking place throughout the entire region, spreading outward into additional jurisdictions. While stabilizing to some extent, these diverging trends continue today. By the early 1960s, the city's population had reached nearly 500,000 residents, an all-time high. Thereafter, the number of city residents plummeted, dropping down to under 400,000 people by 1990. That thirty-year net loss of over 100,000 residents would be among the largest percentage decline experienced by other cities around the country in that timeframe. By contrast, the entire region during those decades added close to 2.5 million new people, with only 14 percent by then residing in the city. The city was a noticeably different place.

What might have caused such a swift and severe population decline in a city that had been regarded widely as healthy, stable and an attractive place to live? How did these drastic losses affect the city?

First, most of the tens of thousands of individuals and families who left did not move far, still residing within the region. They settled mostly in the five core counties surrounding the city. In fact, most were still using an Atlanta, Georgia address, and many were commuting into the city for work, services and entertainment.

Second, the incomes of the out-migrants were mostly in the middle and upper economic ranges. As a result, a large slice of the city's tax base to which they had been contributing was lost. They had been customers of the city stores, users of its public and private services, and their children had been in city schools. And most who left were white. At the same time, a number of Black families moved in. Between the arrival of Black families and the loss of white families, the city's racial composition changed dramatically. By 1990, the city's Black population had risen to about 65 percent, while the racial mix in 1960 was almost equally divided by race.

Underlying all of these demographic shifts were laws and practices that incentivized suburbanization, through federal, state and county laws and tax incentives. These legal and economic advantages, of course, were not limited to Atlanta but universal, gutting the whole of public infrastructure in cities across the country.

Some identify these as *push* and *pull* influences for most white people to leave the city. The *push* factors reflected a concern that many white residents felt with the serious decline in the quality of the city's physical attributes, services, safety and general living conditions. Scores of school buildings had aged and were now antiquated and neglected. Some were abandoned due to the loss in the youth population. The park system, already recognized for its shortage of adequate public open space, needed considerable maintenance, greater cleanliness and increased security. With the rapid decline of much of the white middle and upper class and the negative impact that had on the city's tax base, lack of the public funds needed to deliver a high quality of life was sorely felt.

These were factors certainly. But any analysis must also acknowledge the impact of racism as a motivating factor. The resistance to efforts to integrate the historically segregated city was increasingly apparent. More than a few white residents were uncomfortable with, and even hostile to, mixing with Black people in retail stores, restaurants, bathrooms and police units, at sports matches and on buses. Many white parents strongly opposed having Black children enrolled in their previously segregated schools. They argued euphemistically that integration diminished their "freedom of association."

Meanwhile, accompanying these *push* factors were those that served to *pull* people from the city and into the suburbs. The period was one of rising incomes for many, mostly white residents, which produced greater mobility. The postwar period saw increases in marriages and in birth rates, and young white couples found that the suburbs offered new opportunities for satisfying their desires: plenty of new and affordable dwellings, better living environments, more housing space and room for a second car, all of which were available almost within sight of the city. Additional jobs were being added, as well as shopping malls with national retail chains, more branch banks and arterials that improved their mobility. Suburban home mortgages for white families were available at rates of 90 percent or higher, with small down payments—an availability not conveyed to Black families. Underpinning the suburban wave, the main economic beneficiaries, the auto, oil and real estate industries, maintained intense marketing campaigns that attained their sought-after purpose.

This was in clear contrast with what was being offered in the city, now majority Black, where banks would not even consider lending in many parts of the city. When they did, they charged high loan rates accompanied with large cash down payments. Instead, trapped by racist zoning codes and redlined out of financial and insurance markets, Black residents settled where and how they were able, which was generally in core cities.

American culture had changed utterly, an outcome where the lever of stoking racism contributed significantly.

These *push* and *pull* factors played a major role in the decisions made by most of the 100,000, mostly white people, who left the city. Whether those who moved from the city were swayed more by one or another of these factors is a matter of some disagreement. Regardless of the cause, the impact of carrying with them their business, daily purchases in retail establishments, professional service customers, banking transactions, financial contributions to civic organizations and the like negatively impacted the city. But perhaps of even greater significance was the city's loss of its traditional, mainly white leadership. Moving away were lifelong commitments to civic activities, churches and school sports teams, all of which had added to both the public and private good as perceived by the white community. Replacing the formal, largely white leadership model with a more representative leadership model took time. Many years passed before arriving at a degree of collaboration, termed by Andy Young as the "Atlanta Way," a sort of partnership of white and Black business leaders.

Finally, the diminishing city tax base was a consequence of the outmigration. The city's ability to deliver the same level of public services was negatively affected. The city was obliged to reduce the number of public employees who managed and maintained its assets, affecting infrastructure, parks, schools, roads, other facilities and services. In prior decades, federal funds had been available to help cover some of these expensive demands through the late 1970s. The Reagan government, however, sharply curtailed grants to cities, further accelerating the suburbanization wave.

From the Olympic Era Forward

It is important at this point to clarify our references to the distinction between the city and the region, as this distinction dominates the issue of growth, economy, race, culture and politics from the Olympic era on. So, when we refer to the political jurisdiction of the core city of Atlanta, we use the phrase "City of Atlanta," and when we are discussing the region, we use "Atlanta Region." And then use of the single term "Atlanta" refers to the combined metropolitan area. It is also important to set the context for our story, not only looking at the larger urban area but also examining the perspective of almost twenty-five years from the Atlanta Olympics in 1996. One main focus of the book is to chronicle the preparation, staging and immediate effect of the games from a perspective of both halves of the story (the Games and the city), for the first time here told as a combined narrative. But the other focus is the effect of the Games on the city and the region from the today's perspective. One way to do this is to paint a broad demographic picture of Atlanta from 1960 to today, and this is illustrated in Figure 1, which gives some insight into the effect of the Games in 1996 in this continuum as a baseline for the discussions that follow. Here one can see the remarkable continued growth of the region compared with the fairly constant size of the city. Today, with the region now over 6 million and counting, the city is growing slowly toward half a million, now about 8 percent of the region's population, down from about 12 percent in 1995. Even with this steady climb, there is an obvious spike in the 1990s at the time of the Olympics. A closer look reveals that the city itself had lost 20 percent of its population by 1990, but today it has regained that population. Moreover, the percentage of non-white

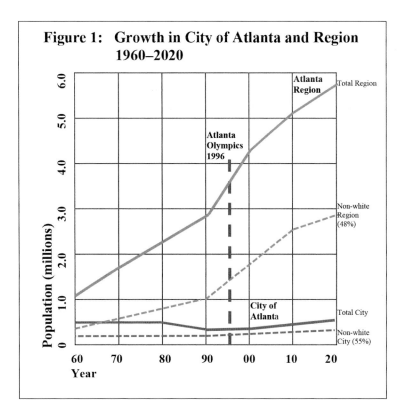

Figure 1: Growth in City of Atlanta and Region 1960–2020

population in the region has witnessed a dramatic spike from about 20 percent in 1990 to 48 percent of the region today, while the percentage of non-white population in the city has actually dropped in the period from about 63 percent in 1990 to 55 percent today as the city has regained population. The non-white population in both areas has also seen a rise in Asian and Hispanic populations, and the 2018 median family income of the city of about $65,000 is beginning to approach about $70,000, although the city still has a significantly larger percent of the population below the poverty line (about 20 percent) as opposed to the region (about 10 percent). All this begins to show that, while in 1990 the region was seen as a mostly poor Black inner city surrounded by booming white affluent suburbs, it now shows the city and even the region emerging together as a major multicultural urban area.

Something clearly changed in the 1990s, and that transformation is still taking place. Yes, the economy boomed in that decade, the growing millennial population began flocking to the city in large numbers and there was a spike in the continuing migration of a Black middle class to the city, all seeking a more diverse urban-centered life. But that also meant that something signaled that it was now okay to return to a city that had been plagued by white flight and urban decay up until that time. Over the intervening years, the city and the region have been emerging together as a major multicultural urban area, shifts that clearly trace their beginnings to the Olympic era.

Census estimates for 2018 show the Atlanta metropolitan area to be the third fastest growing in the United States, the same rank it held in 1995. The city boasts the world's biggest airport and one of the nation's most robust hotel and convention industries. The Peachtree Corridor's "Ridge of Privilege" is still a bastion of a white-centered business investment. Atlanta is known as the birthplace of Dr. King's civil rights movement and has been guided by majority Black political leadership since the early 1970s.

GOVERNANCE

In 1973, Atlanta citizens voted to change their form of governance and adopted a new city charter, as mandated by the Georgia General Assembly. Thereafter, all executive functions were removed from the city council and transferred to the mayor, who would now have the authority to administer all of the city's departments and components. At the same time, the charter changed the boundaries of city council electoral districts, making them more equal in population. With the proportion of the city's population becoming increasingly Black, the white community began to realize that it was only a matter of time before Atlanta became a majority Black city, a transformation that occurred over the 1970s.

The rapid growth in the city's Black population, together with the effects of emerging civil rights legislation nationally, opened up the opportunity for previously denied Black leaders to seek positions of political power. With the new city charter in place, a racial turnover of those holding public office occurred in 1973, with the election of Maynard Jackson, then president of the city council, as mayor. He thereby became the first Black person to head a large southern city. Six Black community leaders joined the twelve-member city council, where only one had held such a position before. (It should be noted that a white person won the tiebreaking position of city council president.)

As a result of these changes, the role of the Downtown white business community, which had essentially controlled city government since its beginning 117 years earlier, changed. The transition in the city governance, replacing white political leadership with Black, presented challenges and difficulties throughout the first four years of Mayor Jackson's administration. Beginning to climb out of the deep and historical breech between the races had and still has a long road to travel, but Jackson's mayoralty marked a major turning point. After Mayor Jackson's two terms, Andrew Young was elected mayor in 1981. His ascension to the mayoralty marked an accommodation and coordination of white-Black leadership that came to be termed the "Atlanta Way," accepted at the leadership level and continuing today. Young played a decisive role in securing the Olympic Games for Atlanta. With the reelection of Jackson as mayor in 1989 to a third term, the city embarked on a better integrated effort to become host of the 1996 Olympics.

This book describes how Atlanta's private and public sectors went about planning and producing the Games and how they followed up in the years following to fuel the city's rapid economic and population growth. It traces how the urgency of being ready for the Games forced Black-white and private-public accommodations to meet Mayor Jackson's commitment to realize benefits for the city at large and especially for those in greater need. It lays out how the city built on the forced partnerships that delivered the Olympics to change public development policy, planning and financing to support continuing collaborations. It then describes how these new arrangements succeeded, or not, in delivering a number of projects whose roots trace to their beginnings in the Olympics moment. We believe that we show that the Olympics provided the "little big bang" that caused positive effects to ripple out from Olympic Ring ever since, not only with *what* was built but with *how* it was accomplished.

1

HOW ATLANTA GOT THE GAMES

An Unexpected Decision

Olympics Background: The Modern Olympiad

The quadrennial Summer Olympics has now become one of the world's largest continually held peacetime gatherings. Its modern version, except for postponement during and after World War II, has continued for almost 120 years. Furthermore, its scale is overwhelming, with millions of spectators and thousands of athletes. Though the event is widely criticized for its many excesses, it continues to captivate worldwide attention.

Originating in 776 BC, these first competitive events were staged at a place now named Olympia, Greece, and then continued in various locations until AD 393. Some 1,500 years then passed. Well into the late nineteenth century, a group of European leaders occasionally met to discuss renewing the Games. At one of these gatherings, a French educator, Baron Pierre de Coubertin, took an active interest. He established the International Olympic Committee in 1894 and began to travel the globe seeking the participation of nations and agreement that, regardless of their sovereign differences and long-standing feuds, they would come together and use sports as a means to restore the competitive and collegial spirit of the early Games.

It was in Athens, Greece, that the modern Olympics first took place to honor the ancient Games. Funds were raised, and 241 athletes from 14 countries gathered in Athens on April 6, 1896, to participate in 43 events before a joyous crowd of over 100,000 persons. As head of the IOC in 1894

Olympic Cauldron and Rings at entrance to Olympic Stadium. *CODA Archive.*

and then as the titular leader of the first Olympics in 1896, de Coubertin was acknowledged to be the father of the modern Olympic Games.

Leaders supporting the effort to restore the Olympics agreed that the event should take place every four years. Athens sought (and lost) to be designated as the Games' permanent home, and the second Olympics took place in Paris in 1900. Starting in Europe, cities around the world have hosted the Olympic Games in subsequent years. In 1924, the Winter Olympics were instituted, also on four-year cycles, with a two-year offset from the Summer Games. On the eve of World War II, the 1936 event took place in Berlin, in Nazi Germany, but the quadrennial events scheduled for London in 1940 and Helsinki in 1944 were canceled for the duration of the war. After the war, the Games returned to their four-year schedule, staging the events in the cities that had lost out due to the war, London in 1948 and Helsinki in 1952.

Meanwhile, the IOC made the noteworthy decision to spread the Games' locations more internationally. They occurred in Melbourne (1956), Rome (1960), Tokyo (1964), Mexico City (1968), Munich (1972), Montreal (1976),

34

Moscow (1980), Los Angeles (1984), Seoul (1988), Barcelona (1992), Atlanta (1996), Sydney (2000), Athens (2004), Beijing (2008), London (2012) and Rio de Janeiro (2016). They were set to occur in Tokyo in 2020 and are projected for Paris in 2024 and Los Angeles in 2028.

How Atlanta?

Almost from its very start in the mid-nineteenth century, Atlanta has drawn leaders in search of civic and universal enhancement. Increases in population attracted their attention, as did growth in investment, competitiveness with other southern cities, receptiveness of newcomers, expansion of its boundaries and economic development. These newcomers expressed their confidence in their prospects and then often a pride in their accomplishments. Over time, this culture became part of the city's very nature. Therefore, when the suggestion was first made that Atlanta should consider hosting a Summer Olympics, the idea was not lost on local businessmen. In the past, the city successfully held large gatherings that had drawn attention to the opportunities to live and work there. In particular, Atlanta, together with six southeastern states, co-sponsored the 1895 Cotton States and International Exposition. That event had two stated purposes: to foster trade between Atlanta and the six states with northeastern and western businesses, as well as with South American nations, and to present Atlanta as representative of a new South, now removed from an unfavorable past and emerging as an important regional commercial center, one suitable for investment and for doing business.

It was an athlete and sports enthusiast, Dennis Berkholtz, who first raised the notion of Atlanta vying to host the Olympic Games. Having played on the American handball team in Munich (1972), he brought with him knowledge of the Games and what the International Olympic Committee would be looking for in a host candidate. His proposal resonated a strong appeal to some key business and political leaders. It also drew the attention of the *Atlanta Constitution*, one of two major local newspapers. To examine the proposal more closely, Research Atlanta, a well-respected local research organization, agreed to assess his proposal's feasibility. Its report, however, was not favorable, especially in light of the large financial losses that Montreal had recently incurred from its unfortunate experience in hosting the 1976 Games. After that, support for Berkholtz's proposal slipped away.

The stories about what happened next are many and rich, characterized generally here. In late October 1986, Atlanta attorney William "Billy" Payne read in the morning newspaper that Nashville, Tennessee, was considering making a bid to host the 1996 Summer Olympics. In his football-playing days at the University of Georgia, Payne had excelled—he was chosen as an All-American lineman—and after college retained a strong interest in sports.

He wondered about why Nashville would even think in such global terms. Then the thought occurred that Atlanta would certainly make a very good choice. At the time, the city contained about 400,000 residents and falling, quite a bit fewer than many of the great world capitals that had previously hosted the Olympics. The city, though, was the center of a region of almost 3 million people. But Atlanta, Payne knew, had a long history in professional athletics and its airport was one of the busiest in the world, sending planes each day to the far reaches of the globe. The region also had a number of global businesses such as UPS, Delta Airlines and Home Depot, with Coca-Cola and CNN in Downtown. Payne increasingly began to feel that his city might make a serious run to draw the 1996 Games. He spoke to leaders in the community as well as those with long-term experience in sports operations. Becoming convinced of the idea, he took a leave of absence from his law firm and formed the Georgia Amateur Athletic Foundation (GAAF), a not-for-profit corporation whose mission was to bring the Olympic Games to Atlanta.

While Payne garnered only moderate support for his idea initially, he turned to several close friends—later known as the "Atlanta Nine"—whom he persuaded to help him develop a bid that could go the United States Olympic Committee (USOC). That organization had the responsibility to select America's candidate to seek the 1996 Games, and that was to be Payne's target as a result.

Among those from whom he sought early advice was Andrew Young, who at the time was the mayor of Atlanta. Atlanta had played a central role in the American civil rights movement of the 1960s. Young had been a close aide and companion to the movement's leading voice, the Reverend Dr. Martin Luther King Jr. Subsequently entering politics, Young was elected to represent a U.S. congressional district whose boundaries included a major portion of the city. He later served as the U.S. ambassador to the United Nations under President Jimmy Carter before becoming mayor.

Payne brought the Olympic proposal to Young, not simply to seek his backing but also to enlist his help in establishing a vision. Young's role as U.N ambassador provided him broad knowledge on countries throughout the world, a crucial component for mounting a bid. Young's advice was both positive and of major importance. Developing and underdeveloped countries, he felt, would be drawn to Atlanta's role in that history. Payne also knew that Young would have an influential effect on his efforts. Although Atlanta's city government was not directly involved in the bidding effort at the beginning, it later officially endorsed Payne's plan on the condition that it would not cost the city any money.

CHOOSING AMERICA'S CANDIDATE

In September 1987, Atlanta submitted its bid to the United States Olympic Committee headquarters in Colorado Springs, Colorado, along with thirteen other American cities. In Atlanta's formal presentation to USOC officials, Payne and others from the GAAF stressed Atlanta's history and background in sports activities and its existing professional and college facilities available for the competitions. He committed to underwriting any needed new construction. In addition to the presence of sports facilities, Payne pointed to the city's extensive airport connections, an exceptional capacity for accommodating large gatherings, the fifty thousand existing nearby hotel rooms and a modern rapid transit system. In addition, the city was a center in the worldwide network of television facilities, including CNN, whose headquarters was located in Atlanta's core, where major venues would be placed. The bid described Atlanta's long history and leadership in the civil rights movement and mentioned that it was the first large southern city to integrate its public facilities. Finally, the bid referenced Atlanta's experience and ability to raise private funding from large corporations and foundations. This was deemed to be of particular importance, since little money would be expected to come from federal, state and local governments. Payne's team presented a video titled *Live the Dream* featuring Georgia governor Joe Frank Harris, Mayor Young and Martin Luther King III, the son of the civil rights leader, reflecting local and diverse racial support for the Olympic initiative.

From the list of fourteen cities, the USOC narrowed the number of competing cities down to two: Minneapolis–St. Paul and Atlanta. Both cities made their final presentations to the USOC's 102-member executive board meeting in Washington, D.C., in April 1988. On April 29, 1988, the USOC selected Atlanta as America's candidate to host the 1996

Olympics. According to interviews with members of the Atlanta Organizing Committee (AOC), the organization that succeeded that GAAF, Atlanta's bid won out based on its excellent organizing ability, venues, hotels, airport and rapid transit system, as well its ability to handle masses of people. They also commented on Atlanta's enthusiasm, the diversity of its leadership and its essential backing from top political and financial leadership.

Until then, few residents of the city had given much attention to the efforts of less than a dozen Atlantans who were seeking the Olympics, and even fewer of these residents felt that there was a serious chance that the Games would actually come to Atlanta. With the news, that speculation changed immediately. Excitement over the announcement soared, and questions were forthcoming: How did all this happen? Who else was seeking to host the event? What were the chances of being selected? When would it be here? And then the incredulous, "Why Atlanta of all places?" Suddenly, reporters from distant newspapers, magazines, television networks and wire services flooded the city.

These were not, however, the paramount questions on the minds of many of the city's leaders. They were concerned with the city's recent negative publicity on the unrest and turmoil around the murder rate and particularly national coverage of the city's "missing and murdered children" crisis. This, together with the decline of city resources to maintain the public infrastructure—streets, sidewalks, parks and utilities—all in great need of attention. Would the wanting physical conditions found in several neighborhoods close to the city's center be an embarrassment? And what would prevent negative social conditions from spilling out to threaten the multitude of visitors? Millions of people would be drawn to the city if it was chosen to host the Games. The amount of time remaining to address this long-standing neglect amounted to just eight years.

PREPARING THE BID

Given the short time available before Atlanta's bid to the IOC was due, 1989 and 1990 became crowded with activities and set on a fast track for accomplishment. Juan Antonio Samaranch y Torelló, IOC president and longtime sports administrator in his native Spain, visited Atlanta to familiarize himself with the status of Atlanta's program. He observed possible competition sites and paid special attention to the degree of community support, an element the IOC deemed important. To build public backing, the AOC launched an all-out publicity campaign that succeeded in rapidly building up awareness, support and anticipation for the next stage of the competition, competing with other finalist cities.

BASIS FOR THE CHOICE

The IOC's work toward the selection process, scattered across the globe, is both demanding and unpredictable. Members spend years traveling, meeting and becoming familiar with candidate cities. The IOC judges each city on both its capacity as well as its anticipated attendance. While Atlanta was a relatively small city at 400,000, albeit in a region of 3 million, the IOC estimated the Games' attendance at 6 million. In Atlanta's bid book, answers based on Payne's initial representations to the USOC to the questions of capacity and capability are synopsized in the following categories: transportation, access, accommodations, communications, Eastern Time Zone, media center, culture, cultural program, sports and opportunities.

Atlanta's transportation assets highlighted the airport as the busiest airport in the world, with direct flights to most of the nation's and the world's destinations. In addition, it had direct, in-terminal rapid rail access to the city's major commercial destinations, including most of the high-capacity venues in the Olympic Ring. In addition, the city was described as the hub for major north–south and east–west interstate highways, all of which converge in the city center.

Its access assets centered on the Metropolitan Atlanta Rapid Transit Authority (MARTA), which again served most of the destinations for participants and visitors, with the promise of using expanded bus service to fill in the blanks.

As the major convention and sporting activities concentration in the Southeast, Atlanta boasted fifty thousand hotel rooms with more to come, again the preponderance of which were either in or within eight miles of the Olympic Ring.

As the headquarters of CNN, the city had long been a media hub, hosting other major national events like the 1988 Democratic Presidential Nominating Convention. In addition, with its extensive fiber-optic network, it provided access to all of the other major broadcast and telephone service corporations, and it was the headquarters for the BellSouth telecommunications giant.

Its location in the Eastern Time Zone positioned it well as the most densely populated time zone in the United States as well as more or less amenable broadcast viewing times in Europe (five hours later), South America and the U.S. West Coast (three hours earlier). And the bid promised a major state-of-the-art media center.

As the home city of Martin Luther King Jr. and the locus of the Jimmy Carter Center, the city's rich and diverse cultural heritage would hold appeal for a wide audience of prospective visitors. Its array of galleries, theater offerings, dance and music companies along with its emerging centrality in the worlds of hip hop and rap were examples of the range of cultural experience on display in the core and throughout the city. The bid promised a comprehensively thought-out program highlighting and expanding on its already existing cultural assets, termed the Cultural Olympiad.

As mentioned, Atlanta had a long history of competing for and attracting major sporting events of all kinds, bedded at the time in nationally dominant university sports teams and professional major league teams. In short, the city had in place organizations that knew how to host major sporting events. And the bid promised a major move to reach out and connect to youth sports activities throughout the city and the region.

The AOC's plans and programs for the Games called for spending $1 billion. That would include $418 million for construction of an eighty-five-thousand-seat stadium, an aquatics center for swimming and diving, a water polo stadium, a track cycling venue, a shooting range and an Olympic marina in Savannah, Georgia, among other projects. Twin dormitories for the Athletes' Village were included at a cost of $60 million. Proposed sources for revenue would come from broadcast television rights, fees, corporate sponsorships, ticket sales, Olympic coins and other merchandise. In contrast to the funding of previous Olympics, little taxpayer money from the federal, state or local governments sources was anticipated.

The bid documents stressed the transformation of Atlanta as it was trying to become one of the country's more racially integrated communities. The leadership of Billy Payne, a white man, with his tireless planning and advocacy, and Mayor Andrew Young, a Black man, with his credentials as President Carter's UN ambassador, known and respected worldwide, symbolized Atlanta's effort. In this vein, the documents noted the city's civil rights progress, imparting a feeling that fueled a strong sense of civic optimism and a desire to make a difference in global matters.

SUBMITTING THE BID TO THE INTERNATIONAL OLYMPIC COMMITTEE

Atlanta submitted its bid to the IOC on February 1, 1990. Five thick volumes of materials sought to introduce IOC members to Atlanta and its people. The submission presented welcoming messages from Georgia's public and private leadership. It gave a full description of AOC's extensive plans for holding what might become the largest peacetime event in history.

The five other invited cities also submitted their materials before the due date of February 12: Athens, Greece; Belgrade, Yugoslavia; Manchester, England; Melbourne, Australia; and Toronto, Canada. Melbourne's bid was made in conjunction with Stockholm. From the outset, many conceded that, since the 1996 Olympics would be observing the 100th anniversary of the modern Olympiad in Athens, the Greek city would be a strong favorite for the award. In addition, as excellent as Atlanta's credentials were, since Los Angeles had just hosted the Olympics Games in 1984, some felt that another country should be awarded that honor.

Atlanta chose several priorities to guide its campaign efforts. The highest of these was the need to build greater recognition of the city since it would not be known by many members of the IOC. Some might have passed through its major airport and knew Atlanta only as having been the birthplace of the legendary Dr. Martin Luther King Jr. or remembered the role that the city had played in the film *Gone with the Wind*. But these bits of knowledge would hardly qualify it for such a momentous event. In addition, among recent hosts, few had occurred in a city as small as Atlanta. Certainly Athens would qualify for its long and distinguished history.

Volume 1 of the bid documents captured the city's attractiveness: its impressive natural environment, gardens, abundant tree cover and rolling landscape; modern architecture and historic places; and examples of its vibrant economy. It showed the area's numerous educational facilities, religious buildings, commercial structures and centers of entertainment and shopping. Volume 2 gave a brief history of Atlanta and Georgia. Then it described the city's Civil War destruction and burning in 1864 and its rising from the ashes, symbolized by the phoenix, to build a modern metropolis. The documents described plans for ACOG's Cultural Olympiad, as well as the proposed torch relay, which would pass through all of the former host cities of the modern Games. Volume 3 gave ACOG's answers to the nineteen specific questions posed by IOC to all five of the competing cities. Volume 4 described in detail all of the sports venues, while volume 5 addressed how the media would be accommodated.

Introducing Atlanta to the World

During almost eight months, from early February 1990 until the day of the announcement of the host city, the Atlanta Organizing Committee continued its frenetic campaigning schedule, locally and globally. An Atlanta team, led by Charlie Battle, traveled extensively around the world, speaking of Atlanta and its attributes, making personal contacts with IOC members, international sports officials and local leaders.

Anxious to familiarize IOC's members with the city, an Atlanta delegation attended IOC's Executive Board and the ANOC General Assembly meetings in Barcelona preceding that city's own Olympics. The International Baseball Association hosted the World All-Star Amateur Baseball Game in the Atlanta–Fulton County Stadium.

Local, state and national business leaders met with IOC members to assure them that there was sufficient financial backing to accommodate the AOC's ambitious venue construction program and other Olympics costs. The AOC placed primary focus on the youth of Georgia with the initiation of the Olympic Day in the Schools (ODIS) program. Organized and chaired by volunteers, the program provided curriculum guides to help teachers incorporate Olympic values into all subject areas. The program culminated the following year with Georgia Olympic Day, where students across the state competed in academic and athletic contests in the style of the Olympic Games. Throughout the seven years of the ODIS period, more than one million young people participated in the programs.

Prior to the IOC's Ninety-Fifth General Session in San Juan, an AOC delegation led by Payne presented a technically sophisticated interactive video that allowed viewers to "fly" through three-dimensional scenes of Atlanta as well as computer-generated models of existing and soon-to-be-built facilities. IOC members and 160 international media representatives experienced that video, produced in association with the Georgia Institute of Technology (Georgia Tech) in Atlanta.

In June 1990, at the IOC Executive Board and ANOFC General Assembly in Barcelona, Atlanta learned that it was to present its credentials to the IOC members when they were to meet in Tokyo in September to choose the 1996 Games host city. Atlanta's Mayor Maynard Jackson also presented an ambitious Olympic Development Program that the city would undertake to realize short- and long-term benefits that the city would seek from hosting the event.

By the September IOC meeting in Tokyo, Atlanta had drawn sixty-eight IOC members to visit the city, a significant number. In addition, Atlanta's AOC representatives had traveled to the homes or homelands of eighty-five IOC delegates in seventy countries.

ANNOUNCING THE WINNER

More than three hundred Atlantans and Georgians traveled to Tokyo to hear IOC's decision on the 1996 host city. They included a group known as the "Dream Team," fifty-eight enthusiastic and diverse students, whose average age ranged from eleven to eighteen years, all wearing straw hats.

With the closing of the doors to the meeting, presentations began with Atlanta speaking first. Its hour-long program included a film and original song, titled "The World Has One Dream." Andy Young, Billy Payne, Mayor Maynard Jackson and Governor Joe Frank Harris gave talks, each seeking to communicate the message from the people of Atlanta and the state of their aspirations to host the Games. The five other cities followed with their own presentations. Then, after clearing the room of nonmembers, the IOC took the first votes.

In all, the member body voted five times. The plan was that following the first round of voting, the city receiving the fewest number of votes would be eliminated. Then a second round of voting proceeded in the same manner, then a third if one city had not drawn a majority of votes. Then if only two cities remained, a final vote would be taken and the city with the most votes declared the winner.

At the end of the fourth round, only Athens and Atlanta remained in the running, and the atmosphere was charged. On the fifth and final vote, Atlanta, which had been steadily gaining additional votes with each round, was declared the winner by a vote of 51 to 35.

The doors opened, and President Juan Antonio Samaranch y Torelló stepped to the microphone and spoke the awaited words: "The International Olympic Committee has awarded the 1996 Olympic Games to the City of...[pause] Atlanta." With that announcement, the Atlanta contingent in Tokyo broke into jubilation. People began jumping up and down, hugging one another, holding their heads in disbelief. The long nine-year effort reached its ultimate reward.

It was 7:30 a.m. in Atlanta, and a crowd of thousands had gathered in Underground Atlanta, a commercial plaza downtown, listening in the cool dawn for the news. When it came, noisy excitement rang out throughout the city from people who had risen early to sit in front of their television sets, hoping for good news. And when it came, there was great joy. By 9:00 a.m., the *Atlanta Constitution* has distributed its paper with the front-page headline reading "IT'S ATLANTA!" printed in huge, bold type.

ACOG—Managing the Preparations

IOC required the USOC to form an organizing committee within six months following the announcement that Atlanta would host the 1996 Games. The less formal Atlanta Organizing Committee then reconstituted itself into the Atlanta Committee for the Olympic Games (ACOG), legally incorporated ten days after Atlanta's selection. ACOG had the responsibility of fostering a national and international amateur sports competition and organizing and conducting the Games.

A thirty-one-member board of directors was established to approve ACOG's programs, policies and financial investments. Its membership included U.S. IOC members, the president of USOC and representatives from AOC, USOC, local governments, the Atlanta business community and communities hosting the venues. The board chose as co-chairs Mayor Andrew Young and Robert M. Holder Jr., a local businessman. The board named a nine-member executive committee to approve ongoing operational duties, such as adopting an Equal Employment and Opportunity Plan, putting forward a code of ethics, managing the preparations of the venues and disseminating ongoing information about the preparations for the Games.

The board adopted a mission statement to guide ACOG's program and operations in all planning and decision-making. Its mission read:

- "Conduct the Centennial Olympic Games with sensitivity, integrity, fiscal responsibility and commitment to the needs of athletes;
- Share with the world the spirit of America, the experience of the American South, and the vision of Atlanta; and
- Leave a positive physical and an indelible mark on Olympic history by staging the most memorable Olympic Games ever."

Here follows our summary of ACOG's final report on the Games. The board's management structure called on Payne to report directly to the board of directors. He had launched efforts to bring the 1996 Olympics to Atlanta, oversaw the initiative and, with others, brought in the political and business support as well as the financial resources sufficient to hold the Games. Payne thus had the primary responsibility for all aspects of the Games, directly managing all functional areas. This included planning and putting on the ceremonies, managing governmental relations and working with the USOC to oversee the efforts of the merchandizing arm, the Atlanta Centennial Olympic Properties (ACOP). In addition, he would manage community relations, oversee the Cultural Olympiad and organize volunteer services and youth activities. For outreach, he would develop the education and communications strategies; his goal was to leave a proud physical legacy.

A.D. Frazier Jr., the chief operating officer, reported to the CEO on finance and accounting, construction of new facilities and operation of the Games. Frazier created functional departments, including managing directors and divisions that would have designated responsibilities in the areas of sports, technology, construction, accreditation, international relations and venue management, among others. In all, seven departments and divisions reported to Billy Payne, and twelve other functional areas reported to Frasier.

Early on, the IOC began to take an active role in defining its relationships with ACOG. It established two commissions: the Coordination Commission, to review and periodically report on the preparations for the Games, and a Centennial Commission, which would ensure that this, the 100th anniversary of the Olympic Movement, would be appropriately commemorated. The former met twice yearly with ACOG's management, while the latter met in June 1994 in Paris during IOC's 103rd session. Standing commissions of the IOC were to provide direction and guidance for their ACOG counterparts, including management for sports and ceremonies, radio and television and medical services, particularly as related to drug testing and facilities for the care of athletes and other Olympic family members.

ACOG began to work closely with the twenty-six International Sports Federations (IFs) that were especially engaged in ensuring that the grounds, tracks, courses and equipment conformed to rules. They also were to verify all results before their release to the media. The National Olympic Committees (NOCs) began working with ACOG to ensure that their teams' housing and services were well provided for in the Olympic Village and the accommodations sufficient for the number of athletes still seeking qualification to compete.

In the United States' role as the host country, USOC participated extensively in the 1996 Games. They retained a management function through their representation on the ACOG Board of Directors. USOC and ACOG also formed Centennial Olympic Properties, a joint venture that was responsible for marketing, sponsorships and granting licenses of official products. It helped raise a substantial portion of funds needed to stage the Games. Finally, under the Tri-Party Agreement, the city set up the Office of Olympic Coordination, headed by Susan Pease Langford, which reported to the mayor and ACOG. Its function was to facilitate agreement between ACOG and city departments on the substantial number of issues and activities that needed addressing, including those related to how to share operating costs, providing law enforcement support and managing sanitation and traffic.

In July 1992, a delegation from Atlanta attended the ninety-ninth meeting of the International Olympic Committee in Barcelona, Spain, in the wake of that city's successful Olympics hosting. Included in the delegation were Billy Payne; Mayor Jackson; George Berry, president of MAOGA (more about this later); and William Hybl, president of the United States Olympic Committee. Payne's remarks covered the status of the Games, while Mayor Jackson presented Atlanta's Olympic Development Program and the initiatives Atlanta and others would undertake to implement the plan.

Beginning in 1994, the emphasis in ACOG turned to implementing and testing the various aspects of the plan to ensure timely and satisfactory delivery for the staging of the Games. They combined a master scheduling system with a budget review system that allowed progress to be measured and budget data to be continually updated.

ACOG's utilization of volunteers proved to be essential. Volunteers worked in all areas of operation based on the needs of the functional areas and the volunteers' availability, flexibility, willingness to fill an identified need and skills. A call center was set up—it received several thousand calls each day to ACOG offices—staffed entirely by volunteers. In 1992, after the internal volunteer program's first year of operation, approximately 300 individuals were participating consistently. By April 1996, the number had grown to more than 800, as the individuals assumed their Games' volunteer positions. Over the five-year period, volunteers devoted 542,000 hours to preparations for the Games. The total number of people with direct hands-on experience, including volunteers and employees, was 53,540.

MAOGA

Early on and long before the Tokyo meeting, Payne began reaching out to secure the support of public agencies and private entities that would need to participate should Atlanta be chosen to host the 1996 Games. As one example of partnership, on December 22, 1988, following an earlier meeting, he wrote to Tom Lewis, special executive assistant to Governor Joe Frank Harris, expressing the need for the state to create a State Olympic Authority. The purpose for the authority would be to enable the state to enter into contracts with the Atlanta Olympic Committee, the U.S. Olympic Committee and the International Olympic Committee. (The city itself could not enter into such agreements under various statutes.)

On April 21, 1989, the General Assembly of Georgia unanimously created the Metropolitan Atlanta Olympic Games Authority (MAOGA). Governor Joe Frank Harris was quoted in press accounts as declaring: "The idea of having the Olympic Games in Georgia has widespread support throughout the state. These bills demonstrate both our state's commitment to amateur sports and the determined efforts of Atlanta's business and community leaders to win the Olympic Games." The purpose of the authority was to sign a host city contract and provide state oversight for the 1996 Centennial Olympic Games.

The January 25, 1991 Tri-Party agreement set forth the divided responsibilities among the City of Atlanta, MAOGA and ACOG. Three weeks later, on February 6, 1991, MAOGA adopted an Equal Employment Opportunity Plan and Code of Ethics. Provisions of the code barred Olympics officials from accepting favors, gifts or loans from anyone seeking Olympics business, sharing insider information, using their association with the Olympics to gain special privileges or taking a job that would be in conflict with official Olympics duties. The mission statement, which MAOGA adopted on March 1, 1992, read as follows:

> *In cooperation with the Atlanta Committee for the Olympic Games and others, to assure that the 1996 Centennial Olympic Games are the most successful Games ever, in conformance with the legal framework of the Act creating the Authority, the Host City Contract and the Tri-Party Agreement, and that the Games result in appropriate legacies for the citizens for the City of the State of Georgia.*

A twelve-person board of directors was established, headed by George Berry as chairman and Marvin Arrington as vice chairman. The authority would contract, on behalf of ACOG, with individual governments and governmental entities that would host Olympic venues. Under its primary oversight role, MAOGA would be engaged in four major activities to complete its obligations: approve venue location changes; review ACOG's budget, financial statements and forecasts; review and approve construction contracts over $250,000; and complete the Olympic Stadium.

In addition, from the outset the authority anticipated that it would support expanding the scope of activities beyond MAOGA's oversight role, utilizing its own broad powers to become a catalyst for projects that leveraged the staging of the games to provide legacies for the State of Georgia. Examples of such projects would include development of single-family housing along the Olympic Corridors and the development of commercial and multifamily housing around the Olympic Stadium.

Notable dates and actions by MAOGA concerning the stadium included the selection of the stadium design team and approval of its guidelines. This took place on July 10, 1992, followed by a review of schematic designs on October 26, 1992; the signing of the stadium agreement on March 16, 1993; the groundbreaking dedication ceremony for the stadium on July 11, 1993; and final approval of the $154 million construction contract on February 2, 1994. The stadium was then prepared for the Games' opening ceremonies on July 19, 1996, and for the closing ceremonies on August 4. In addition, MAOGA also approved the construction contract for the natatorium on Georgia Tech's campus on April 20, 1994, and $15 million equestrian venue on May 20, 1994.

This chapter summarizes how the AOC won the Games for Atlanta and what ACOG put in place for the private sector initiative to go forward. The next characterizes the circumstances faced by the city as a whole at the time of the award and the tasks it faced in order to be ready.

2

THE CITY PREPARES FOR THE GAMES

W ith the IOC's choice of Atlanta for the 1996 Olympic Games, beyond the fanfare and euphoria, city leaders took stock of the city's economic and social conditions and its infrastructure, parks and amenities and found this assessment sobering. Millions of people would be drawn to the city now chosen to host the Games. Bad press, occasional unrest, the deteriorated condition of the Downtown and its neighborhoods (the center for most of the venues) all had to be improved to avoid embarrassment. Perhaps most sobering was the question of funding: would there be enough time and money to address these long-standing needs and neglect?

ATLANTA IN THE EARLY 1990S

From one perspective, residents of the Atlanta metro area in 1990 might well look back and admire the changes of the previous three decades. Its population had tripled, making it a metropolis of three million people. The airport had developed a global reach, the primary roads formed an impressive network of interstate and arterial highways and a rapid rail passenger system had recently been launched. Located within the region's boundaries were the Georgia State Capitol, the National Center for Disease Control and Prevention and the headquarters of such corporations as Delta Airlines,

Centennial Olympic Park. *EDAW, INC.*

Coca-Cola, Home Depot, the Southern Company and then, in 1992, United Parcel Service. There were highly regarded educational institutions, such as Emory University, Georgia Institute of Tech, Georgia State University and the Atlanta University Center, the largest center for historically Black colleges and universities (HBCUs) in the nation—Morehouse, Spelman and Morris Brown Colleges, Clark Atlanta University, the Morehouse School of Medicine—as well as Interdenominational Theological Seminary. In addition, the city housed an impressive array of cultural and entertainment centers, museums, historic collections, theaters, the opera, the ballet, a major symphony and vaunted sports organizations. Most of these resources were located in the core of the city, a benefit for citizens and visitors from beyond.

The city also had much to celebrate in its progress in improving race relations. Recent decades had seen many major legal barriers standing between closer relationships in the Black and white communities struck down, and the city had become a national center for the civil rights movement. This improvement was visibly evident with the successive elections of Maynard Jackson, Andrew Young and then again Mayor Jackson.

In 1988, the Democratic Party held its national presidential convention in Atlanta. Major league sports had arrived with the National League's Braves team. The Georgia World Congress Center greatly expanded in 1978, and the city ranked among the country's top three sites for conventions. Visitations were on the rise, as people came to extol the beauty of the neighborhoods and flowers of great variety, all under a heavy tree canopy throughout the year. When most thought about Atlanta, it was one of America's fastest growing metropolises, the location of major sports teams, recognized voices on national issues, national Black leadership and a handful of Fortune 500 corporate headquarters. Atlanta appeared to clearly economically dominate an entire large region of the country.

Some would conclude that with these assets the City of Atlanta must have had a booming economy. A closer look, however, would reveal that many of those huge enterprises and public works had been built and operated in the larger region for the most part with corporate monies and federal and state resources. The City of Atlanta had funded only a small part of these investments, and the direct financial contributions had been minimal. These private and public entities and infrastructure investments contributed much to the region, and the city gained considerably from their presence. Yet the city's budget was inadequate to support the needs of many of its citizens, two-thirds of whom had incomes below 80 percent of the area median income and were nominally eligible for receiving federal Community Development Block Grant funding.

From this perspective, for many residents, especially African Americans, life in the city had not been easy. Within a three-decade period, from 1960 to 1990, the city had lost over 100,000 people, predominantly from the white middle- and upper-income classes. In leaving, they took with them major commercial businesses, daily economic activities, significant professional services and, importantly, a considerable portion of the traditional white civic leadership. The city's economy, accordingly, suffered from a declining tax base. Reduced resources led to significant cutbacks in the maintenance of schools, parks, infrastructure and other public facilities.

Low- and low middle–income neighborhoods and their inhabitants, mostly African American, experienced the brunt of this decline and its attendant inattention. The result was deteriorated housing, breakdowns in the infrastructure, high unemployment rates, a paucity of jobs and widespread poverty. Over these decades, news about the city's difficulties was widely spread. A story in the January 1977 issue of *Harper's Magazine* listed Atlanta as one of the nation's worst cities, based on statistics of crime, poverty and health insurance. In 1978, federal officials declared that the city had the highest crime rate in the country. Others had cited it as the country's homicide capital. From 1979 to 1981, Atlanta suffered a shocking spate of child murders known nationally as the Atlanta Child Murders. A series of articles in the leading local newspaper, the *Atlanta Constitution*, was titled, "City in Crisis."

These conditions suffused the deeply embedded social problems that the city was facing. Then, on April 29, 1988, the United States Olympic Committee chose Atlanta over thirteen other cities to be the country's representative to vie for bringing this high-profile international event to the country in 1996.

Once the initial thrill eased, however, sober heads had a different understanding of the demands that would fall on the city. Given the city's current fiscal, economic and social state of affairs, would the city really be able to host such a huge global event? The Atlanta Organizing Committee, the group planning to sponsor the Games, already had grand plans that, when followed, would be able to produce the competition itself, plus all of the ancillary happenings associated with the event. The USOC was likewise satisfied that the capacity of the present convention halls and transportation system could accommodate the events. Excellent sports facilities already existed to house many of the events, and the AOC committed to building the Olympic stadium as well as other necessary venues. In addition, the city's ability to handle the large demands from its convention business—supported by the hotels, restaurants and other private ventures—was truly impressive.

Yet many knew that recent decades had left the city's public infrastructure untended, especially its streets, sidewalks, parks and plazas, most badly in need of maintenance and additions. Visitors had long noted the visual quality of the city was lacking in grandeur, both in its architecture and its public realm. And perhaps most importantly, many lamented the poor quality of the physical conditions and social dismay found in neighborhoods close to the city's center, where many of the largest venues would be located. Would that not reveal the downside in Atlanta's stated affairs? Millions of people would be drawn to these areas if Atlanta was to be chosen to host the 1996 Olympics. Would the city's serious social problems—drugs, panhandling, petty crimes and harassment—seep into the large crowds of visitors? And given the limited resources available to the city already burdened with its own financial malaise and with only a few years left to address these problems, could the typically polarized political and business leadership come together to adequately confront and alter these realities?

MOVING TOWARD RECOVERY

In 1990, Maynard Jackson returned to the mayoral office. He was not facing the best of times. Two weeks before his inauguration on January 5, Eastern Airlines, the city's second-largest airline and eighth in the country, already in bankruptcy after being plagued for years by management and labor disputes, stopped flying. One month later, its assets were liquidated, including valuable routes to Miami, the Caribbean and Latin America. Then came another setback, both economic and psychological, when Rich's, an iconic Downtown department store, closed its doors. Although its large outlet on the northern edge of the city remained open, that did little to ameliorate a wide sense of despair. Morris Rich founded the store in 1867, only three years after a Civil War battle had virtually leveled the city by fire. For the next 124 years, the store had anchored the city's commercial heart and become one of the country's largest department emporiums. Its closing created not only deep sadness, but the loss also brought full attention to the sharp decline in the retail sector occurring in the core of the city. Many in Atlanta faced difficult economic and institutional declines. To one interviewer, Jackson said, "When I left office, there was no crack [cocaine]." Now, he continued, there was "crime, guns, dope, lack of values, lack of direction among those who are caught up in the dope world, communities being undercut." On top of these indicators of economic decline, real estate development, a bulwark of the city's economy, was declining everywhere but in the northern community of Buckhead.

SETTING THE OLYMPIC COURSE

Such were the challenges Mayor Jackson carried with him to Tokyo on September 19, 1990, when the International Olympic Committee announced that Atlanta would host the 1996 Games. Upon his return, he put together a program of actions that the city would need to take to be prepared for what would become the largest event in its history.

He made three assignments. John C. Reid, the city's chief operating officer, was tasked to assess what effect the Games would be expected to have on city personnel, services and costs. The mayor then appointed his assistant Cecilia Corbin Hunter to serve as the liaison between the city and the Metropolitan Atlanta Olympic Games Authority—the state organization that would oversee the construction of the Olympic Stadium and Natatorium—and ACOG, as well as other organizations and entities that would play a role in the Olympic preparations. For the third position, Jackson was seeking someone who would oversee the planning and development needs of the city, anticipate changes in those needs and establish a long-term vision to ensure that current decisions would be compatible with realizing that future and support it. For this position, Jackson turned to Leon Eplan, primary author of the first two chapters this book.

Two weeks after the September 18, 1990 of Atlanta in Tokyo, I received a 6:00 a.m. call from Maynard (he always started at that early hour). He was inquiring if I would agree to return to the City to help begin its readiness for the Olympics. (As you know, I had previously served as Maynard's Commissioner of Budget Policy and Planning.) I was overwhelmed by his offer since I regarded that a call from the city's mayor to undertake such a responsibility is no small request. It was a planner's dream! So I immediately told him I would be pleased to join with him on this extraordinary venture. I immediately changed the course which I had been following for a few years. It took me all of two weeks for me to close down most of my consultant contracts, and another two to move to City Hall and meet with my new employees.

Additional weeks followed when I next met with the Mayor and the COO, John Reid. At that meeting, I told them (as they knew), that the huge scale of the Games will produce unprecedented demands on the city's workforce and its management capacity as well as also enhance considerable financial resources and new funding opportunities. Also, and at the same time, we certainly realized that the Games would unleash an enormous increase in public energy as well as provide considerable opportunities for citizen involvement and participation. All of these would also enlarge benefits beyond anything we had ever realized in the past. As such, I told them that we needed to develop the means to "capture" whatever benefits we can and begin to do so now. We should choose to spread our efforts across much of the city: much grander, larger impact, greater number of rewards. And we needed to begin to do this now. Fortunately, I said, my department already processes the very capabilities that would be needed to capture the benefits as well as the training required. These capabilities had been derived from our putting together the city's annual comprehensive development plans in coordination with the 24 city-wide NPUs [Neighborhood Planning Units]. *Furthermore, it is important that we recognize the increase in the number of benefits which will accompany this largest of events, the coming of the considerable economic, social, physical diversity, the introduction of different cultures and languages, the emphasis on our additional knowledge of the world. All of this would be needed to develop a process for "capturing" these new and very different benefits produced by the Games and direct them to confront several problems that had been working against the best welfare of the city.*

*Both Maynard and his COO concurred with the recommendations I was making and wanted me to develop further details. This was what I began to do, starting with assigning a few of the staff to operate under Director of Planning Fernando Costa. I assigned them to put together a full development program for the Olympics and to determine an organizational structure to achieve what we were proposing. In time, much of the Atlanta Olympics Development Program that evolved was passed on to CODA and other contributors.**

Eplan had served as Atlanta's commissioner of budget and planning during the mayor's first term in office, 1974 to 1978. Having worked with the mayor during those four years, he was familiar with the actions he wanted to take on behalf of the city. He was also familiar with the city's departmental administrative operations, structure, procedures and legislative processes. The department he was now to administer, however, had changed. He would become the commissioner of planning and development. As the city's former planning commissioner, he would be returning to his previous position but also administer the city's Bureau of Buildings, a unit that approves all building plans and certifies the construction of all commercial building, inspects changes made and undertakes all building code enforcement.

As described earlier, Atlanta entered the 1990s having suffered through three decades of distress and decline. More than 100,000 residents, mostly white and middle-class, had moved away during the period from 1970 to 1990, primarily to the suburbs. Throughout these thirty years, citizens pressed the city to address shortages of adequate, affordable housing and employment for thousands of individuals and families, primarily Black residents with lower incomes. Many of these communities had also been displaced by expressway construction and urban renewal project clearances. In addition, there were thousands of migrants coming to the Atlanta region

---

* Leon S. Eplan, Atlanta Olympic Development Program, Department of Planning and Development, City of Atlanta, Georgia, notes from 1991.

from parts of Georgia and elsewhere, a result of urbanization and the South's rapidly shifting rural economy. The effect of these events—the loss of much of the white middle class, many businesses and the tax base along with the displacement of residents due to public construction projects not offset by immigration from rural communities—was spread across the three decades and severe. Most important to Jackson, these net declines in population and the city's income levels negatively affected the tax base, making the city less able to maintain its infrastructure, schools and parks as well as employ and retain an adequate workforce.

Seeking ways to remedy Atlanta's unfavorable state and its many social issues, like homelessness, while still improving its citizens' expectations for its future, Jackson turned to the Olympics as a rare moment to address the city's stagnation. Billions of dollars would be allocated over the next four years for new buildings, athletic facilities and the operation of the Games, and tens of millions more would be spent by visitors. The challenge was to find a way to redirect some portion of these monies toward projects and programs to increase employment, rehabilitate neighborhoods, rebuild an aging infrastructure and improve the city's tax base. Eplan was given the responsibility of putting together an Olympic Development Program that would serve the demands of the Games; address the city's social needs, weak economy and infrastructure decline; and, at the same time, move the area toward a brighter future.

Such a goal would not be unique. Several past Olympic cities had tried to use the occasion to make immediate and long-term improvements. Most of these, however, fell short, with venues going unused and the momentary boost leaving mixed legacies at best. The 1992 host, Barcelona, however—recovering from the oppressive reign of dictator Francisco Franco (who died in 1975)—began planning for the Games on its award in 1986. It set out to rebuild its long-neglected physical environment, neighborhoods and housing; upgrade the utility systems and transit; construct a beautiful park along its waterfront; restore its plazas; and relocate its central railroad line from the center of the city. In effect, Barcelona sought to transform itself into a modern city that could more readily compete with other great urban centers of Europe, an effort that was largely successful. How could Atlanta learn from Barcelona, and how could it set up a program that could help achieve positive results for its citizens?

As the Olympics preparation effort began to ramp up, however, still other events continued to plague Jackson's early tenure. In May 1992, the city suffered a serious riot in the wake of the Rodney King decision in Los Angeles. Four officers had been caught on tape as they beat King, a Black taxi driver, after a high-speed car pursuit. The officers, none of whom was Black, were accused of assault with a deadly weapon and exercising excessive brutality. Six days of widespread rioting and substantial looting led to fifty-three deaths in Los Angeles and a national debate on police brutality and racial injustice. In Atlanta, a group of about one thousand Black youth stormed into Underground Atlanta, an enclosed Downtown commercial center, turning over merchandise carts, breaking store windows and threatening patrons. Once outside, they threw rocks, looted several stores, overturned trash cans and benches and accosted white bystanders, one beaten almost to death. By nightfall, local police had arrested about three hundred rioters, and for days after, the city was shaken.

Despite these setbacks, the early 1990s marked the nadir of the city's long period of distress. While its difficulties received widespread coverage in the media, the city began to rise out of its weak post–World War II state of affairs and move toward its long-sought upward goals, as enumerated in the succession of Comprehensive Development Plans that Jackson initiated in his first two terms. Recognizing how deep and pervasive these problems had been, Jackson assigned additional police to patrol high-crime neighborhoods. He turned to outside expertise to coordinate multiple public agencies and for advice on ways to improve public services such as removal of garbage, vacant properties and other civic deficiencies prevalent in low-income areas. The city's economic development agency began to funnel information to community leaders regarding available job opportunities. The city's Neighborhood Planning Unit (NPU) system, which Jackson and Eplan established in his first administration, was tasked with providing feedback on problems in local communities. Later in the 1990s, the Atlanta Housing Authority increased its efforts to replace public housing projects with mixed-income housing and neighborhoods.

Then, assistance to address some of the city's most serious physical and social issues appeared, somewhat unexpectedly, from three sources: the Carter Center's The Atlanta Project, the U.S. Department of Housing and Urban Development's Empowerment Zone program and activities taking place as part of the efforts to win and then host the Olympics. These initiatives supported and overlapped and interconnected with the Olympic Development Planning (ODP) Program that Mayor Jackson called for.

THE ATLANTA PROJECT

In 1991, the Carter Center, former president Jimmy Carter's organization in Atlanta, launched an effort aimed to ameliorate some of the city's poverty-related problems. The Atlanta Project would take advantage of the president's considerable experience in dealing with similar problems around the world, as well as his ability to raise funds. This five-year $33 million effort would, in time, become one of the largest privately funded anti-poverty programs in the country. Its target was a large cluster of neighborhoods located primarily in Atlanta's southeast, where three-fourths of its residents were African American and unemployment stood at over 25 percent in a city with a 5.6 percent overall rate. Programs concentrated on the high rate of infant mortality, school dropouts, assistance to households (of which well over half were headed by single women) and a scarcity of skilled jobs. At the forefront of all its activities, and the issue of most immediate concern to residents, was addressing violence.

What characterized The Atlanta Project work was an assurance that residents would define and help prioritize their needs. Thousands of volunteers were recruited to help make the process successful. To briefly summarize a few of its initiatives:

- Major local corporations, banks, social agencies, universities, federal agencies and others committed up to a full year of their time and provided professional expertise and in-kind services and supplies.
- A leading bank began free check cashing for residents in public housing projects, along with assistance in setting up bank accounts.
- With seed money from The Atlanta Project, six banks and the Atlanta Chamber of Commerce launched an $11.5 million program designed to make business loans available to budding entrepreneurs who might not otherwise qualify.
- A housing resource center was established to support community development projects.
- Of considerable importance, ten major federal and state agencies worked together to simplify and consolidate sixty-four common application forms for public assistance into an eight-page document.

- The U.S. Forest Service and Georgia Forestry Commission, with the assistance of paper companies and local green groups, helped residents plant trees and promote environmental education programs.
- In just a week, twenty-seven thousand children received immunizations.

The Atlanta Project did not remedy all of the city's decades-long social needs, but it marked the beginning of the recognition on the part of its traditional civic leadership that the city's racial and social injustices were unsustainable. Some 25 percent of the city's citizens needed attention, not continued neglect, and they had to become engaged to guide processes that would meet needs on their terms to improve the situation for those in need to launch improvement strategies across the city.

The Empowerment Zone Program

In 1993, Bill Campbell, with the support of Maynard Jackson and Andy Young, was elected mayor, and he presided over the city's implementation and aftermath of the Olympic Games. Following up on The Atlanta Project, in 1994 his administration applied for and received a U.S. Department of Housing and Urban Department (HUD) grant as one of six cities chosen to receive funds under its new Empowerment Zone Program. Between 1994 and 1998, HUD set aside $100 million in grant monies and $150 million in tax benefits to the recipient cities to achieve their primary goal of revitalizing economically distressed areas. The designated zone encompassed thirty-two neighborhoods generally around the city's center, in southeast Atlanta, some of which had also participated in The Atlanta Project. Efforts fell into five major program areas: economic development, adequate housing, safe and livable communities, lifting youth and families out of poverty and establishing public participation strategies. During the program's eight years, tens of millions of dollars and tax credits flowed into the zone. Major initiatives included home ownership assistance programs, treatment for pervasive asthma, fire protection measures in homes and apartments throughout the area and the preparation of citizen-guided neighborhood development plans for all the neighborhoods.

Unemployment rates fell by a small percentage as average incomes and home ownership increased. Private investment experienced a tentative spread into the neighborhoods. Although the margin of success was less than expected, there were clear signs that Atlanta had embraced and at least partially realized the Empowerment Zone goals, including an increase in the level of employment, a reduction in the percentage of vacant housing units, mitigation of fire hazards, reduction of asthma zones and a drop in poverty rates.

The 1994 Infrastructure Bond Referendum and Other Olympic Response Initiatives

After two earlier bond referendum defeats, people's consciousness of the need for funding sources to address Atlanta's longstanding and deteriorating infrastructure initiatives and the onrushing Olympics persuaded citizens to support the 1994 referendum effort. The projects identified were citywide in scope and aimed at some of the worst deficiencies. At the same time, however, many of the priorities responded to infrastructure needs in the immediate Olympic ring area. Though a pittance of what was needed, the awareness of the needs and the will of the people to do something about it signaled a change in attitude and in governmental response, in which the Olympics was a focusing moment.

The Atlanta Project, the Empowerment Zone and the bond referendum were successive moves on the part of city government to implement Mayor Jackson's visions for implementing the Olympics in a way that could actually benefit the city's citizens. ACOG aided Atlanta's efforts to achieve its desired turnabout. For five years, the organization sponsored local events that contributed to growing anticipation about the coming event. Thousands of residents thundered through a five-thousand-meter run, placing colorful banners heralding the coming Games on streetlight poles. Olympic-related programs were prepared and introduced in schools and were shown on national television. ACOG also underwrote productions held at Atlanta Symphony Hall as part of the Cultural Olympiad.

Public ceremonies honored visiting dignitaries from around the world; international athletic meets were convened at the Atlanta-Fulton County Stadium. ACOG alerted the media to groundbreakings for the Olympic Village at Georgia Tech, the Olympic Stadium in Summerhill, a gymnasium at Morehouse College and an outdoor stadium at Clark Atlanta University.

ATLANTA'S SELF VISION

It was clear to Eplan that Atlanta's Olympic Development Program (ODP) would draw its activities from the city's current Comprehensive Development Plan (CDP). In Mayor Jackson's first term in 1975, Eplan created the planning and neighborhood engagement strategy that would now guide the ODP. Under its charter, the city was mandated to produce annually a comprehensive plan at one-, five- and fifteen-year intervals, in which NPUs had an advisory role.

The CDP works according to the following parameters. Once the Department of Planning and Development and its collaborative partners complete the draft plan, it conducts a series of public hearings and televised presentations. The department then sends the draft package to the mayor for his/her preliminary approval. The mayor then forwards the plan to the city council, which holds its own public hearings, amending the plan as it sees fit, before adopting it by ordinance for the mayor's final approval. Thereafter, during the coming year, the plan serves as the legal policy statement on all city development and can be altered only after holding scheduled quarterly hearings. Any modifications proposed at these hearings must be approved or denied by both the city council and mayor.

An important part of the approval process is the input the plan receives from citizens. The city charter requires that the public must be given a means for participating in the plan-making while it is being prepared. Rather than this becoming an ad hoc process, citizen involvement in Atlanta is firmly structured, with notices of meetings for review sent well in advance. To facilitate citizen review, the city has been permanently divided into twenty-five neighborhood planning units, established in 1974, that annually elect their own officers. Each NPU unit meets monthly throughout the year to express opinions on proposed public and private developments as well as the comprehensive plan, which are then transmitted to Planning and Development and the city council. These are usually discussed at the following NPU meetings, and if the unit so chooses, its advice and presentation is sent to the Zoning Review Board. Ultimately, a request for a change in the CDP is made to the city council for final approval or denial.

THE OLYMPIC DEVELOPMENT PROGRAM

Atlanta was satisfied and legally comfortable with having its Olympic Development Program rest heavily on the 1990 Comprehensive Development Plan, the year when the IOC selected Atlanta as the 1996 host city. It had undergone, as described, extensive review by citizens and city departments, followed by public hearings and approval by the mayor and city council. Finally, with the adoption ordinance passed by the council, projects and programs from the plan could then be readily selected for implementation. The CDP's one-year projects, for example, were already built into the programs of city departments, with several already in the Department of Public Works' agenda. However, time for implementation was critically limited. Less than four years remained in which to choose the projects and have them authorized, designed, constructed and tested before opening day. It was to be a race against the clock.

The city's projects and programs for the 1996 Games moved through a four-step decision process. The first two steps were taken directly from the adopted 1990 CDP. First, the *Vision* for the future set the entire agenda. The second step used the plan's same four *Goals*, all of which were deemed valuable in giving the Vision needed specificity and guidance for decisions and actions. The third step, related to the Games themselves, established its own *Objectives*, different from those in the CDP, all four of which gave more direction for the actions intended to serve the identified demands of the Olympics. And finally, from these Objectives, *Plans*, *Projects* and *Programs* were chosen as specific projects expected to either be completed or be underway by July 19, 1996, the opening day of the Games.

VISION STATEMENT

Getting to Atlanta's Vision Statement was rooted in the understanding that the Olympics event represented a means and a catalyst for realizing the city's desire for its future. As indicated, Jackson viewed the Games as a unique opportunity to address some of the most important issues facing the city and prepare for the challenges the city would face for much of the remainder of the twentieth century. Broadly, the city was to become a stronger center of an increasingly diverse region and take on the status of a global city. To move toward that vision, the city adopted three goals, with supporting objectives.

1. Undertake actions which would lead the City towards a more humane, safe and enjoyable place to live, work and raise its children. To accomplish this, the City would need to:

- *Increase the abundance, quality and accessibility of parks, plazas and open spaces and increase the funding required to build and maintain the quality of public space.*
- *Provide greater opportunity for pedestrian movement by means of new and improved pedestrian-ways, then increase use and availability of sidewalks, and achieve better access to public and private properties.*
- *Enhance the visual quality and beauty of the City through widely valued architectural styles, an increase in the amount of landscaping, use of varied materials, clearer information, greater sensitivity to human scale, and protection of valued urban vistas.*
- *Secure the City's irreplaceable historic heritage and cultural life.*
- *Expand and protect Atlanta abundance of its natural and manmade environment in order to achieve a healthier and more wholesome existence for residents and visitors.*
- *Provide a safe environment for the protection of life and property for residents and visitors.*

2. Establish a more integrated, multi-modal and diverse transportation system which would move people and goods in a more efficient and environmentally sensitive manner. To accomplish this would require that the City:

- *Increase efficiency and conservation by encouraging greater adherence to comprehensive, continuous and cooperative transportation planning and implementation.*
- *Assure a better balance among the variety of modes to move people and goods. While the majority of citizens and visitors will continue to move by automobile, it is apparent that other modes must be realized and utilized to a far greater extent than at present, and to give riders greater choice among alternatives. That requires deemphasizing movements of people by rail, including MARTA, streetcars, people-mover systems, commuter connections throughout north Georgia, and respond to the approaching high-speed rail networks.*
- *Build all systems and alternative modes so as to have minimal adverse effect on the quality of residential life and on the natural environment.*

- *Increase the efficiency of existing streets and arterials through the utilization of better traffic management technologies and higher levels of maintenance.*
- *Provide for safe and efficient operation of Hartsfield Atlanta International Airport as Atlanta's port for international and domestic air travel.*

3. Raise the productivity quality of life of all citizens, thereby enhancing their enjoyment of living in Atlanta. As Atlanta begins to grow again, retain its more intimate development scale which would, as it has in the past, encourage people to relate to and get to know and understand each other. Unfortunately, the gap between the prosperous and disadvantaged continues to widen. It must be recognized that far too many Atlanta residents remain poor, live unproductive lives, and are not participating in the coming growth and prosperity. Addressing this problem must become the City's highest priority.

- *Protect, maintain and enhance the quality of neighborhoods through stronger development regulations and environmental controls, and balanced growth policies and an emphasis on small parks, passive open spaces and greenway linkages.*
- *Support greater neighborhood cohesion and empowerment through programs designed, with resident involvement, to raise the viability, living standards and levels of human service delivery in disadvantaged and aging communities.*
- *Promote greater economic and human development investment throughout the City, giving attention especially to poorer areas on the City's southeast and west sides.*

At the larger scale, the Comprehensive Development Plan (CDP) enumerated these objectives:

- *build closer relationships with other political entities within Atlanta's expanding region and to regain its role as the central place for coalescing the region's different cultures, people, and lifestyles in its increasingly diverse community; and*
- *link Atlanta with a network of major cities scattered throughout the world as the City assumes the global responsibilities now being placed upon it.*

In July 1992, a delegation from Atlanta attended the ninety-ninth meeting of the International Olympic Committee in Barcelona, Spain. Included in the delegation was Billy Payne, president of ACOG; Atlanta mayor Maynard H. Jackson; George Berry, president of MAOGA; and William Hybl, president of the United States Olympic Committee. Payne's remarks covered the status of the Games. Concurrently, Mayor Jackson briefly presented Atlanta's Olympic Development Program and the initiatives the city and others would undertake to implement it.

PROJECTS AND PROGRAMS IN ATLANTA'S OLYMPIC DEVELOPMENT PROGRAM

The preliminary list of plans, projects and programs for the Olympic Development Program were those that already had been on the city's work list as informed by its Comprehensive Development Plan and accompanying Capital Improvement Program. The projects listed were grouped in three categories to indicate the central purposes of Atlanta's Olympic Development Program:

- projects to serve the visitors who would be coming to the Games from the other parts of the country and from abroad;
- projects to improve neighborhoods affected by the Olympics;
- and projects intended to leave a lasting tribute to the Olympic Games.

The program anticipated that the list would undoubtedly change during the next four years, with some likely added or even eliminated by CODA. It would have to account for factors such as whether they could be substantially completed by opening day, if there would be adequate funding, if public approval requirements could be successfully met and if CODA's projects could be easily coordinated with ACOG's own schedule, among other issues.

ACTIONS TO ACCOMMODATE VISITORS

A large number of improvements were proposed to help support the needs of the projected two million visitors who would visit Atlanta during July and August. That total amounted to over eight times the size of the city's residential population. It would be the largest group that had ever visited Atlanta. As such, the visitors would make extraordinary demands on Atlanta's infrastructure, public facilities and a variety of services needed to accommodate this crowd. Although the requirements for public responses would be spread over the seventeen-day period, every day would command large-scale demands, especially during the initial week. Some of a wide range of improvements would call for temporary arrangements, while others would be permanent and have a lasting effect. ACOG, and private and nonprofit organizations, embarked on a program designed to serve visitors for the Games.

IMPROVEMENTS TO NEARBY NEIGHBORHOODS

Efforts to revitalize these communities had been ongoing for several years, but now, major new investments would need to be considered in their parks, infrastructure, housing, education facilities and programs involving human and social services. Additional funds would also be required to help local communities organize, plan and oversee the rebuilding of their neighborhoods. Of the nine most affected neighborhoods, the communities that would require the most attention were Summerhill, Mechanicsville, Butler/Auburn and Old Fourth Ward.

These strategic initiatives are detailed in the following outline. The projects were designed to ensure that long-term neighborhood improvements would occur well beyond the planned Olympic activities. The Bureau of Planning, under its director, Fernando Costa, identified similar specific projects and initiatives for the remaining neighborhoods, placing particular emphasis on Atlanta University, English Avenue, including Egan Homes, Vine City/ Ashby and Peoplestown and Techwood-Clark Howell.

ACTIONS TO CREATE A LASTING LEGACY

In addition to efforts to accommodate visitors and improve the lives of city residents, the Olympics were expected to help guide the city along the course that it already had set in the CDP and the ODP. The expectations of Atlanta's residents for its future have always been high, both in size and quality.

The physical legacy would be projects that it intended to accomplish in the near term, most of which were undertaken and put in place in time to support the Games, while efforts on the other elements would be completed in the coming years. The activities and energy expected to be unleashed by the 1996 Olympics would be a major influence in all of these efforts.

The conditions faced by the city on Maynard Jackson's assumption of the mayor's office were daunting. The Atlanta Olympics Committee persisted in its unlikely quest to gain the 1996 Olympic Games for the city, a success. The Atlanta Committee for the Olympic Games, as required by the IOC, took on the responsibility, largely privately funded, to put on the event. Mayor Jackson, with his administrative moves and the establishment of the Olympic Development Program, prepared the city to connect the events to each other and the larger city. The program called for bringing lasting benefit to its citizens, especially those with greater needs. The ODP set the program for how to do that. While not all of the actions were completed, it is remarkable how effectively the city met most of its goals. This document set the course for concretizing how to implement Mayor Jackson's vision for the city's Olympic agenda, addressed in chapter 3, and laid the groundwork for the legacy that followed, addressed in chapter 6.

3

TWO PLANS FOR
THE ATLANTA GAMES

I
n 1992, Mayor Jackson put forth a dual agenda for the Olympics. For
Andrew Young and others on the bid committee, the city's task was
to put on a successful athletic event. Mayor Maynard Jackson, on the
other hand, described the challenge as scaling the "twin peaks of Mount
Olympus": one peak was to stage a spectacular Olympics, the other was
to use the games to revitalize inner-city Atlanta. Jackson's more expansive
view raised expectations for what could and should be done during Olympic
preparations and broadened the debate over what hosting the games should
mean for the city's residents.

The management of this dual agenda fell to two distinct entities: the
Atlanta Committee for the Olympic Games (ACOG) and the Corporation
for Olympic Development in Atlanta (CODA).

The Games were mostly privately funded, although, in the end, a third of
the total cost of $3 billion would be made up of a variety of public sources
(see Table 8, page 101). The sanctioned organization for preparation and
hosting activities, ACOG, focused its attention and money on the major events
themselves (see chapter 2). Realizing that needed public improvements were
too much for existing city agencies to handle, Jackson created a nonprofit
corporation to implement the City's Olympic Development Program. The
board of the new corporation, CODA, was large and inclusive, comprising
thirty-six prominent business, public, nonprofit, academic and other leaders
of the city. Co-chairs of the board, Mayor Jackson and developer John
Aderhold, were later replaced by newly elected Mayor Bill Campbell and
Joe Prendergast, president of Wachovia Bank of Georgia. Throughout the

Threshold, sculpture at entrance to Underground Atlanta. *Neil Dent; artist Robert Llamos.*

process and into the immediate post-Olympic period, CODA relied on advice particularly from itts largest funding sponsors, including Prendergast, Ingrid Saunders Jones (a vice president of Coca-Cola) and Curley Dossman (director of the Georgia Pacific Community Foundation).

Shirley Franklin, Atlanta's former commissioner of cultural affairs and later the city's chief operating officer under Mayor Young, was appointed by Mayor Jackson as CODA's first executive director. She was soon replaced by Clara Hayley Axam, former director of the city's Department of Administrative Services under Mayor Young. H. Randal Roark, on leave of absence from the Georgia Tech College of Architecture and Planning, was named as director of planning and design, and planner Stephanie Organ was named director of neighborhood revitalization. Shirley Franklin then became the community liaison coordinator for ACOG, and Jack Pinkerton, a highly respected contractor and a member of the original ACOG bid committee, moved over to become CODA's assistant CEO. These two crossovers provided virtually the only connection between ACOG, the city and CODA as ACOG took a distinctly remote approach to relationships with both city government and citizens alike. Thankfully, both Franklin and Pinkerton stepped up to provide the much-needed lines of communication.

Formation of CODA was complete in late 1992, and the staff was in place by mid-1993 with a startup grant of $1 million from the Woodruff Foundation. No other public or private funds were in place, and no plan of improvements had been adopted. There were now but three years to the start of the Games, and the *Atlanta Journal and Constitution* called CODA "hapless" even before the staff was in place.

The City of Atlanta provided much-needed coordination, oversight and permit management to both ACOG and CODA. Key city leadership in executing the city's Olympic agenda were Leon Eplan, commissioner of planning and development; Cecelia Corbin Hunter, appointed by Mayor Jackson as the city's first Olympic projects coordinator; Douglas Hooker, commissioner of public works; Barbara Bowser, commissioner of cultural affairs. Mayor Campbell appointed Susan Pease Langford to succeed Cecilia Corbin Hunter as the Olympic projects coordinator. Then Hunter was appointed to lead the Paralympic Games.

During this period of organizational "storming," John Reid, was the city's chief operating officer under Mayor Jackson. Later, in 1994, Mayor Bill Campbell appointed Byron Marshall, a professional city manager, as the chief operating officer to succeed Reid. Marshall provided the essential "glue" and consistency that allowed planning to proceed even in the midst of major changes in the political landscape resulting from city elections. Marshall was particularly effective at facilitating the completion of projects in the final months before the Games.

The State of Georgia was also a significant public actor in preparing for the Olympics. Most coordination was managed by MAOGA, the Metropolitan Atlanta Olympic Games Authority, with George Berry as board chairman; Richard Montieth, director; and architect Sara Haga as projects coordinator. MAOGA provided the authority for the use of eminent domain, essential to the work of both ACOG and CODA.

Other major entities were the Georgia Department of Transportation, under the direction of Wayne Shackelford, and the state-owned Georgia World Congress Center, under the direction of Dan Graveline, owner and operator of several facilities that would become Olympic venues and later the primary developer and owner of Centennial Olympic Park.

THE PHYSICAL CONTEXT WITHIN THE OLYMPIC RING

To fully understand the character of the two plans for Atlanta's games one has to look not only at the political and economic conditions in the city in the early 1990s but also at the physical context and unique development within what came to be known as the "Olympic Ring." This was an arbitrarily designated three-mile circle in central Atlanta containing most of the Olympic venues and the city's development program initiatives.

The history of Atlanta's founding and early development was unique in that it was established as a rail terminus for several rail lines in the 1830s converging on undeveloped land in the Georgia Piedmont. The rail function was primary, with the new city developed to serve it. Multiple development tracts were surveyed perpendicular to the adjacent irregular rail lines, creating intersecting grids with no overall plan, a condition that, along with the hilly topography of the Georgia Piedmont, would create circulation problems throughout the city's history. This was particularly true during the Olympics, which had to implement a bus circulation system due to the dispersed venues located away from rapid transit stations, requiring deployment of over 1,200 buses, including over 140 imported buses and bus drivers from other cities to meet the demand, resulting in significant confusion the first few days of the Games.

The areas consumed by rail rights-of-way were substantial to account for several intersecting lines and large service facilities. This created an almost permanent barrier to the west and divided the two halves of Downtown's early development on the north and south side of the main tracks, defining an area which came to be known as the "Gulch." After the Civil War, the city flourished, but the legacy of Jim Crow divided the city into distinct segregated African American areas, mostly poor, on three sides of Downtown with more affluent white areas to the north. The Downtown core would develop along the "Peachtree Ridge" at the highest elevation in the core, thereby containing the most desired sites for business and cultural facilities, and ultimately bearing the iconic name of Peachtree Street. This corridor would define a "ridge of privilege" that can still be seen in the urban landscape today.

Downtown would be further cut off from surrounding residential areas with the coming of the freeway system in the 1960s and '70s. Racial and social divisions were further accentuated by discriminatory zoning practices, and six separate public housing projects ringing three sides of Downtown were built between 1935 and 1955. Additional social disruption came with two large urban renewal areas on the east and south side in the 1960s. The net result of these developments created a Downtown that was an isolated precinct of white privilege but nonetheless a vital mix of commercial uses, with a vibrant pedestrian life and a functioning urban streetcar system serving adjacent neighborhoods.

The central area also contained several universities: the Georgia Institute of Technology on the north, Georgia State University in the center and the nation's largest cluster of HBCUs, including prestigious Spelman and Morehouse Colleges, on the near west side. Each would play an important role in the staging of the Olympics in 1996.

To realize the transformative potential of the Games, there were formidable challenges to overcome. With the steady depopulation of Atlanta's Downtown and midtown areas during the 1970s and '80s, blight forced the substantial demolition of buildings, many of which had been vacant. Most new Downtown office and hotel complexes created enclaves that faced inward with a full complement of amenities within. This further exacerbated the slow but steady abandonment of the pedestrian function of the street and the physical deterioration of the public environment. The disaster of the disruption and demolition of the central core through transportation and urban renewal projects combined with an outmigration of commercial and residential areas to the suburbs along with the demolition of many buildings, most of them historic, resulted in a deteriorating urban

Olympic Ring Area, 1951.

street life and crumbling infrastructure, leaving little of Atlanta's once vibrant Downtown. The major political development of this period was the election of the South's first African American mayor of a large city, Maynard Jackson, which ushered in a broad change in political power in the city as the civil rights generation of Black leadership had come of age

Within this deteriorating urban landscape of the 1970s and '80s, the city would see pockets of new development on the fringes of Downtown that began to reshape the form and identity of the urban core. Much of the new development would be facilitated by Central Atlanta Progress (CAP), a Downtown business organization led by Dan Sweat, who had been the COO for the City of Atlanta under Mayor Sam Massell in the late '60s and then the director of the reorganized Atlanta Regional Commission before coming to CAP in 1972. These new developments would bring sports venues, hotels, convention facilities and finally rapid rail transit to Downtown, all of which would form the core of the Olympic infrastructure in 1996. However, most of this new development was designed as inward-oriented enclaves, which exacerbated the poor connections to public facilities and street life in Downtown Atlanta.

On the near west side, a new zone of development was emerging over the rights-of-way of the rail lines that would contain the Georgia World Congress Center; the Omni Arena, the multiuse development that would soon house Ted Turner's CNN headquarters; and the Georgia Dome stadium, opened in 1991. A little farther west, the area around the Atlanta University cluster of colleges was becoming a new center of African American culture and commercial activity.

On the northern edge of the historic core, John Portman's Peachtree Center formed a new nucleus for the growing hotel and merchandising industry. Farther north in the area called Midtown, Georgia Tech was growing, albeit at the time in keeping with its inward focus and largely commuter campus. The Woodruff Arts Center was emerging as the city's cultural heart, housing the Atlanta Symphony, the Alliance Theater, the High Museum of Art and the Atlanta College of Art within its precinct. And surrounding the Peachtree and Tenth Streets intersection, the counterculture strip provided the most active street life in the city, but the rest of Midtown was rapidly becoming abandoned.

On the east side, Sweet Auburn had lost some of its commercial and cultural vigor to the west side. The construction of the Martin Luther King Center for Social Change, though, which contained the crypt of the slain civil rights leader and the newly designated MLK National Historic District, supported Auburn Avenue as a primary birthplace of the civil rights movement and a destination venue in and of itself. However, the adjacent vast-cleared urban renewal area of Bedford Pine, which shamefully and totally demolished the historic poor neighborhood of Buttermilk Bottoms, struggled to gain market traction as the market favored the rehabilitation and infill of the economically more attractive older white neighborhoods farther to the north and east throughout the '70s and '80s. (In 1973, the Bedford Pine Urban Renewal Area was leased to private bidders who proposed three thousand mixed-income housing units along with commercial and office development but did not recommend keeping the street grid or any of the housing fabric of Buttermilk Bottoms.)

A little farther to the east, rights-of-way for two proposed freeways were acquired and cleared (except for trees), but through significant local opposition, both were halted. Most of both rights-of-way remained under the ownership of the Georgia Department of Transportation until the 1990s, with some lots resold for infill housing. The large cleared area at the proposed intersection of the two freeways immediately adjacent to the King Historic District became the site for the Jimmy Carter Center and the Jimmy Carter Library and Museum, constructed in the 1980s. Together these iconic venues created the opportunity for the Freedom Park and Parkway (now known as John Lewis Freedom Parkway) built at the time of preparation for the Games.

On the south, another large urban renewal project demolished most of the historic Summerhill neighborhood to make way for Atlanta–Fulton County Stadium, which would become the site of the adjacent Olympic Stadium in 1996. The historic heart of Downtown at Five Points attempted, with mixed results, to maintain its prominence with the creation of several projects:

- the "Underground" Atlanta entertainment district beneath the viaducts built over the "gulch" of the rail lines.
- the creation of Woodruff Park via the demolition of a block of historic structures by the Trust Company of Georgia and various Coca-Cola–driven philanthropic sources;
- the insular but growing campus of Georgia State University;
- and the construction of the 5 Points MARTA station, at the junction of the two main transit lines, which opened in 1980.

The rest of Downtown was rapidly becoming a wasteland of vacant lots, parking lots and deteriorating infrastructure. All these developments would fall within the arbitrary circle of a three-mile radius that would define the Olympic zone.

In addition to the troubling physical conditions within the Olympic Ring, even more troubling were poverty levels in the surrounding neighborhoods, deteriorating housing stock and a lack of public amenities. In terms of demographics, Atlanta proper was relatively small (394,017 people) in 1990, according to the U.S. Census Bureau. Its central core was surrounded by several low-income and largely African American neighborhoods. All of this was surrounded by a thriving region twelve times the city's size that exhibited the opposite trends of population and economic growth. By

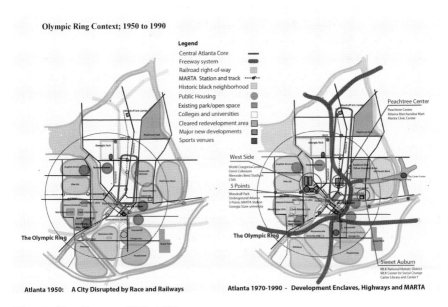

Olympic Ring Context, 1950–1990.

1990, middle-income, mostly white neighborhoods such as Candler Park and Morningside had experienced rehabilitation efforts, while the poorer and mostly Black neighborhoods were yet to experience any movement suggesting transformation.

Thus, at the announcement of Atlanta's winning bid for the Olympics in 1991, the Olympic Ring was made up of diverse urban histories and contemporary political and economic forces that ACOG would have to negotiate both socially and physically. The divisive and heavy-handed interventions of rail and highway development and invasive urban renewal demolition and relocation of residents, all overlaid with the stifling layer of Jim Crow–era legacies, would not be easy to overcome. Into this crucible of widespread urban decay and demolition on the one hand and isolated pockets of new urban life on the other, the Centennial Olympic Games, the world's largest and most visible mega-event with its eight-million-plus visitors, was coming to town.

Given these conditions, it seems that the decision to locate the major part of the Olympic venues Downtown within the Olympic Ring was a bold and risky move. However, the presence of existing facilities, a growing base of hotel and convention accommodations and the MARTA rapid transit system made Downtown perhaps the only choice if the Games were to be mostly privately financed. Thus, the physical plan for the Olympic Ring was limited almost to the choices that were actually made. Existing venues were widely dispersed within the Ring, as little or no additional land was available Downtown. This kept venue sizes limited and would be a challenge for pedestrian circulation and security during the Games.

Between the Olympic venues, longstanding lack of attention to urban infrastructure and pedestrian services throughout the Ring exacerbated the need to adequately serve the Olympics. There was, for example, only one major venue directly connected to the rapid transit system, necessitating planning for vastly improved, safe pedestrian corridors and a significant temporary bus system for both athletes and spectators. This was a different situation than in most of the recent host cities at the time, where most major venues were located in a vast, secure precinct, often away from the central area and thus requiring new or upgraded transit access. Unlike Atlanta, this model could be easily secured while also encouraging ample pedestrian circulation and necessary services.

If the ambitious agenda of the twin peaks was going to work for the benefit of the City, ACOG would have to locate and construct the Olympic venues with a design and investment sensitivity to the surrounding context. And

CODA would have to not only repair and improve the existing infrastructure within the Olympic Ring but also create a new sustainable culture of connectivity between Downtown and the surrounding neighborhoods that Atlanta had never had to weave together. It would have to leverage the diverse human and physical resources into a robust multicultural and multifunctional urban core for the twenty-first century.

In short, would the Olympics be part of the problem or part of the solution for Atlanta's future?

The ACOG Plan: "Inside the Fence"

ACOG's charge was to develop venues, including Olympic Stadium, the Olympic Village and Centennial Olympic Park. As each sporting venue had a security perimeter (festively decorated by volunteers), this was dubbed "inside the fence" work. ACOG also undertook an ambitious community outreach initiative that included neighborhood job training and employment, youth programs focused on various Olympic preparations, the arts-centric Cultural Olympiad and thousands of volunteers.

Venues

The primary sports events would be held Downtown: some at existing, dispersed professional and university facilities, others newly built to the extent possible in existing sports-oriented zones. As many of the venues were within walking distance of, but not adjacent to, MARTA stations, ACOG would enhance permanent and temporary transit facilities along with selected pedestrian corridors to improve connectivity. Housing for ten-thousand-plus athletes was to occupy the entire Georgia Tech campus, creating the largest Olympic Village to date. This urban area encompassing all the Downtown and Midtown venues and related improvements came to be known as the Olympic Ring, a three-mile-wide circle with Woodruff Park at its approximate center.

Fourteen venues were inside the Ring and comprised 62 percent of the total venue capacity. Over half of this capacity was located in existing venues. Other Olympic venues were dispersed outside of Atlanta: six venues were located elsewhere in the Metro Atlanta area and had 21 percent of the total capacity. Five venues, with 17 percent of the total capacity, were located in the broader region. This does not include nearly 300,000 seats located in existing soccer stadiums in four separate cities.

Centennial Olympic Stadium

ACOG's centerpiece athletic venue was the Olympic Stadium. ACOG entered into a creative financing agreement that involved the Atlanta–Fulton County Recreation Authority and the Atlanta Braves major-league baseball franchise. ACOG would build the stadium to Olympic specifications for scheduled events, from the opening and closing ceremonies to the full run of track-and-field competitions. When the Games were over, the north quarter of Olympic Stadium would be demolished and reconfigured to house the Braves. Atlanta–Fulton County Stadium, the existing Braves venue that was to house baseball for the Games, would be demolished after the season to provide parking for the new stadium, named Turner Field for Ted Turner, the team's owner and founder of Atlanta-based CNN.

As the groundbreaking for Olympic Stadium approached, issues of how the existing low-wealth neighborhoods adjacent to the new venue should benefit continued to simmer. Together neighborhood leaders and local unions mounted a campaign to assure residents that jobs and training for people in the affected neighborhoods would be included in the development mix. Their nonviolent actions included sit-ins in ACOG's offices and organizing for a major demonstration. These actions led to an all-night negotiating session

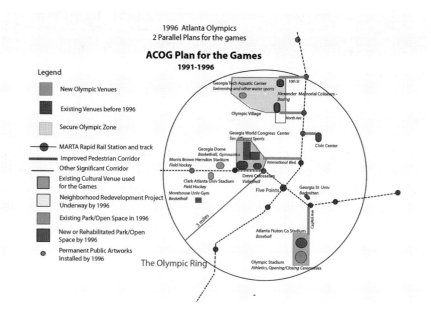

ACOG Plan for the Games.

Olympic Stadium. *Public domain.*

with ACOG's leadership that resulted in the provision of jobs and training for 250 people in need. The outcome transformed the planned protest into a groundbreaking celebration. As an added victory over the development mindset that usually hampers linking jobs for the jobless to large development projects, ACOG agreed to training and employment provisions that did not disqualify the consideration of people with criminal or substance abuse backgrounds, provided they maintained a clean work record.

The Olympic Village

Needing more space for ten-thousand-plus athletes than was available in any contiguous vacant site within the Olympic Ring, the plan was for the

Olympic Village. *ACOG.*

Olympic Village to occupy the Georgia Tech campus of 270 acres, with room to build additional dormitories and the Games' primary aquatic center. All new housing remained following the games to serve dormitory needs of both Georgia Tech and Georgia State University. This new construction of $241 million was jointly funded by ACOG ($47 million) and University System of Georgia revenue bonds ($194 million), which would be paid off by future student rents. In addition, over 1,700 miles of permanent fiber-optic cable was installed within the campus to serve the communication needs of the Games.

Centennial Olympic Park

In late 1993, a little belatedly, Downtown leaders and Billy Payne realized that there was no major outdoor gathering place. To meet that need and to provide for corporate sponsors' giant tents, ACOG and Central Atlanta Progress came upon an opportunity to achieve two goals at once: one, build a grand park, and two, do it by purchasing, clearing and transforming mostly parking lots and small-scale support businesses that separated the major hotels from the Omni Arena and the Georgia Dome. Because of the tight time frame and the need to acquire multiple properties, including one-

and two-story industrial and warehouse-type buildings, ACOG was able to persuade the State of Georgia, through the Georgia World Congress Center (GWCC), to take responsibility for the project. Armed with eminent domain powers, the GWCC was charged with acquiring the property and building, owning and managing the park. To coordinate with the city's agenda, CODA's Roark would facilitate community input and sit on the selection and design review committees. The nationally recognized firm of EDAW Inc. was chosen to design the park, with a team led by EDAW's Atlanta firm leader, Barbara Faga.

The twenty-one acres purchased would become the principal gathering space of the Games. Five and a half million visitors trekked through Centennial Olympic Park during the Olympics, with peak single-day attendance reaching seventy-five thousand. The first phase of construction was completed in just two and a half years in July 1996; the planned second phase was completed in 1998. Centennial Park would prove to be the most visible icon of the Olympic Games.

Cultural Olympiad

The International Olympic Committee requires that all host cities sponsor a festival showcasing the local culture and arts to parallel the sporting events. Starting in 1993, ACOG sponsored the Cultural Olympiad, which culminated in the Olympic Arts Festival. This nine-week festival was held all over the city but centered on the Olympic Village, showcasing the work of more than three thousand artists in over two hundred exhibitions and nineteen public art displays.

ACOG also initiated several ambitious cultural programs that were successful but included only a few permanent legacy projects. These consisted of twelve pieces of public art, five of which are permanent installations, including the Olympic Cauldron. There were also cultural events, including many events from participating countries and held in multiple venues, which began to take place two months before the Games. More than 250,000 tickets were sold to these events, with over 2.6 million attendees. However, some complained that few of the cultural events and sites were planned for lasting effect.

As noted by Michael Lomax in 1997,

From the beginning of ACOG's planning, arts organizations and interest groups acted independently, seeking singular opportunities to collaborate with the Cultural Olympiad. No effective effort was mounted to organize as a community and plan collectively with ACOG. This individualistic and fragmented approach is reflected in the results of the Olympiad itself. Though laudable, ACOG's goals were perhaps most striking for what they did not include, namely, significant plans to construct new facilities or to rehabilitate existing ones, structures that would become a permanent part of Atlanta's, or the state's, cultural infrastructure.

Beginning in 1993, with the staffing of the Cultural Olympiad, ACOG established a mechanism for planning and delivering on its arts and cultural commitments, with three goals for the Olympiad:

- To explore the rich and extraordinarily diverse cultural experiences of Atlanta, the State of Georgia and the American South.
- To present to Southern audiences a variety of distinguished international artists.
- To develop local, regional, and international relationships among artists and audiences and leave behind an expanded vision through which Atlanta may be recognized as an international center of innovative arts, culture, and entertainment.[*]

Community Outreach

ACOG's community outreach initiative included:

- Neighborhood job training and employment
- Youth sports-oriented programs and internships related to Olympic preparation
- Participation in preparation for the Games, particularly in the neighborhoods adjacent to the Olympic Stadium, the Olympic Center and the Olympic Village
- The creation of a ticket fund that allowed seventeen thousand Georgia children from lower-income families to attend Olympic events.

---

[*] Lomax, Michael L. "The Arts; Atlanta's Missing Legacy"; Sjoquist, David L. et al. 1997. "The Olympic Legacy: Building on What Was Achieved." Research Atlanta Inc. School of Policy Studies, Georgia State University.

The City/CODA Plan: "Outside the Fence"

In 1993, by the time the full CODA board was seated, staff put in place and Clara Axam set as the CEO, fewer than three years remained to the opening of the Games. Yet the board decided to pursue both public spaces and infrastructure as well as neighborhood revitalization. In the fall of 1993, the CODA Master Plan, including each of these elements, was adopted following the mayor's agenda and the Olympic Development Plan (see chapter 2). The plan identified $200 million worth of needed projects and established a short-term program of $100 million to be funded and completed by the Games.

There were three main components in the Master Plan:

- CODA would create the five primary pedestrian corridors connecting MARTA to the main Olympic venues;
- CODA and the City of Atlanta would supplement the Olympic agenda with other needed public, permanent improvements that could be "piggybacked" on the Olympic improvements made either inside or outside of the fence.
- CODA would, to the extent possible, pursue improvements to the fifteen neighborhoods surrounding downtown and, in particular, the neighborhoods either immediately adjacent to the Olympic venues or containing a venue within its boundaries.

Public Spaces Program

To accommodate the millions of visitors soon to step inside the Olympic Ring, CODA planned to reconstitute a badly needed pedestrian environment, consisting both of practical infrastructure improvements and enhancements of public art and historic interpretive installations. CODA created a team of architects, planners and landscape architects to act as project directors. The team's goal was to create what they called "connective tissue," a common language of pedestrian amenities in public spaces and corridors, such as streetlights, street furniture, trees, signage and site information. To implement the plan, CODA sought to involve as many professionals as possible, engaging over 120 artists; architecture, landscape architecture and planning firms; and over 75 contractors, fabricators and installers, the great majority being from the Southeast region.

Capitol Avenue, 1996. *Dixi Carrillo.*

Capitol Avenue, 1993. *CODA Archive.*

Atlanta
University
Promenade,
1996, a
pedestrian
corridor
connecting AU
campuses. *CODA
Archive; artist
Brian Rust.*

CODA expanded the five essential pedestrian corridors identified by ACOG to eleven, totaling almost twelve miles, intending to connect Olympic venues and other cultural facilities to the surrounding neighborhoods, connections that had deteriorated through years of neglect or had never existed in the first place. Of particular interest was the improvement of several streets in the area of the Atlanta University campus and a complex of several HBCUs, including a street closure to provide a pedestrian promenade connecting the several campuses.

TABLE 1

CODA Master Plan and Program (completed)	
Pedestrian corridors	11.7 miles
Neighborhood sidewalks	20.4 miles
Parks (new or redeveloped)	8
Public artworks	55
Street trees added	2,400
"Atlanta" streetlights added	1,736
Note: When combined with trees planted by Trees Atlanta Inc., over 10,000 street trees were added to the Olympic Ring by 1996.	

Source: CODA Master Development Program Plan, 1993

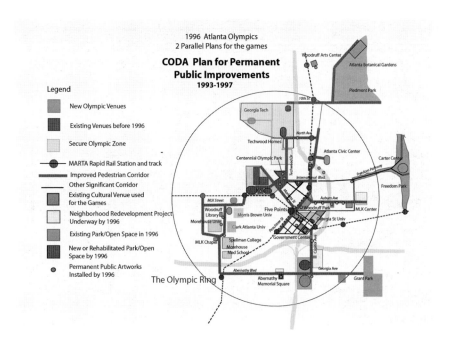

CODA Plan for Permanent Improvements.

As it turned out, CODA performed beyond expectations. Downtown Atlanta, it should be said, has long been a strangely alienating place. All told, it is safe to say that American downtown had devoted less attention to pedestrian amenities and traditional public gathering places. Obviously with this as a context, almost anything could be seen as an improvement. But, thanks to CODA's leadership, Atlanta did a lot more than the minimum.*

Public Arts Initiative

CODA's public arts initiative led to the commission and installation of separately commissioned fifty-five pieces of public artworks, located across twenty-four sites, most of which marked and interpreted some of Atlanta's significant people, places and events. Of significant interest were:

- monuments to five early civil rights leaders along Auburn Avenue, including John Wesley Dobbs, the unofficial mayor of Sweet Auburn, by artist Ralph Helmick;

---

* Benjamin Forgey, *Washington Post*, 1996.

Carnegie Pavilion, a monument to universities in the Olympic Ring, created from the recovered façade of the Carnegie Main Library of 1901. *Neil Dent.*

Homage to King at entrance to Martin Luther King Jr. National Historic District. *Dixi Carrillo; artist Xavier Campegny-Medina.*

Folk Art park, *Homage to Passaquan*. *Neil Dent.*

- a monument to Martin Luther King Jr. by artist Xavier Campegny-Medina, one of six artists from Barcelona, the host of the 1992 Olympic games;
- a monument to Ralph David Abernathy by artist Emma Amos in the Mechanicsville neighborhood;
- the Folk Art Park; twenty-two installations by prominent folk artists on two "left over" parts of freeway bridges downtown;
- and the Carnegie Pavilion, a monument to the presence of nine institutions of higher learning within the Olympic Ring, reconstructed on Peachtree Street in Hardy Ivy Park from components of the Beaux-Arts Carnegie Library, built in 1901 and demolished in 1977, and saved largely through the efforts of COO George Berry and then chairman of the Atlanta Urban Design Commission Randal Roark.

Supporting Public Improvements

While the parks and public art initiatives were the most visible components of the CODA public spaces program, other components were important additions to the public landscape. To make Atlanta history more visible in an environment where the architectural record had largely vanished, over 150 historic markers of various kinds were installed, over half of which were in African American neighborhoods, primarily in Sweet Auburn and the Atlanta University area. Also installed were over 50 pedestrian maps and signs, 29 of which contained historic interpretive panels, in a downtown were there were almost none. And often overlooked were the practical improvements to the pedestrian landscape, particularly with the installation of 1,700 new streetlights and 2,400 trees across 12 miles of fully reconstructed streetscapes and 20 miles of neighborhood street and sidewalk repairs (see Table 1). In such a once thoroughly decrepit pedestrian landscape, to the casual observer this would appear to be a drop in the bucket, but the CODA initiative to re-pedestrianize downtown Atlanta had been jump-started.

CODA's new and enhanced public spaces seek to create spaces to enjoy, to commemorate our unique heritage and to help bind us together as citizens of a city which values its public environment. These public spaces include pedestrian corridors, bikeways, civic parks and plazas, public market areas, and neighborhood street improvements. Wherever possible they have been designed to act as a catalyst for public and private development in adjacent areas. CODA's public space mission also includes reinvigorating the public realm by telling the story of the City's recent past and its continuing development as an international city. To this end CODA is including an ambitious public art and historic interpretive component to its public spaces program, which includes 52 separate artists' commissions across 24 site installations.

Neighborhood Revitalization Program

At the outset, CODA set forth to determine what could realistically be accomplished in the fifteen Olympic Ring neighborhoods prior to the Games. It was obvious to CODA's board and staff that significant brick-and-mortar improvements could not be implemented in the three scant years before the Olympics, and the funds anticipated by Mayor Jackson for this initiative, particularly from the private sector, would not be forthcoming by 1996. Nevertheless, the ambitious program adopted by CODA was vigorously pursued.

---

* Roark, Randal. *The Civic Trust*. The Corporation for Olympic Development in Atlanta, 1995

Local college students helped take a detailed physical survey of conditions in all fifteen Ring neighborhoods (9 square miles and 12,613 parcels, identifying over 11,000 units of substandard private housing units) in the summer of 1993. They then entered the results into a GIS database integrated with county tax records that would be transferred to the city after the Games as an important planning tool. (GIS was not yet widely employed by cities in 1993.)

CODA pursued neighborhood revitalization in partnership with the Atlanta Neighborhood Development Corporation (ANDP), led by Hattie Dorsey, whose primary focus was to develop private and philanthropic resources in designated neighborhoods. By 1996, ANDP had facilitated the creation of twelve neighborhood-based nonprofit Community Development Corporations (CDCs) in the Olympic neighborhoods to complement CODA's focus on planning, public funding and implementation. Early on, CODA's Neighborhood Development program was assisted by

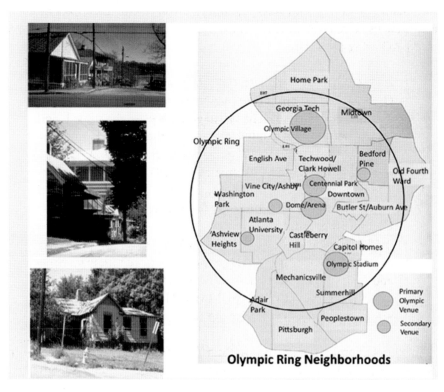

Olympic Ring neighborhoods.

urban redevelopment pioneer Ed Logue, who had consulted with Mayor Jackson's first administration in the 1970s. Logue brought in a longtime associate, architect David Crane, who had been his planning director at the groundbreaking Boston Redevelopment Authority in the 1960s. Crane directed the comprehensive CODA neighborhood survey and remained as a neighborhood redevelopment consultant to CODA.

For at least the four innermost neighborhoods adjacent to Olympic venues—Summerhill, Auburn, Mechanicsville and Old Fourth Ward—complete community-based Community Redevelopment Plans were prepared and legally adopted, and this process would be continued in the post-Olympic period (see chapter 6). In the decade leading up to the Olympics, over $85 million had been invested and over 1,300 new housing units constructed in these neighborhoods (see chapter 4 for details).

CODA began implementing community initiatives identified in the CRP as time and funding permitted. In essence, these initiatives emphasized "doing it right" over "doing it fast" so that the real legacy here was in establishing sustainable processes with full community involvement. Examples of such comprehensive redevelopment using several sources of funds include some of the following projects:

- In Summerhill, adjacent to the Olympic Stadium, the Greenlea Commons mixed-income housing project of seventy-six units and the adjacent Heritage Park were developed, and ten businesses were rehabilitated on the commercial zone along Georgia Avenue. The track-and-field practice venues were built on Georgia Avenue by ACOG and left behind as a neighborhood park. The projects were largely coordinated by MAOGA, the state authority overseeing construction of the Olympic Stadium.
- In Mechanicsville, east of the stadium along Ralph David Abernathy Boulevard, CODA made streetscape improvements and built a plaza and public artwork honoring Dr. Abernathy. The neighborhood CDC, SUMMECH, developed moderate-income rowhouses across from the plaza on Abernathy Boulevard.

In the Olympic Period, more than 3,400 sub-standard houses were demolished, an additional 200 vacant lots were cleaned, volunteers refurbished nearby playgrounds, 280 homes were painted, and Habitat for Humanity, the Atlanta Neighborhood Development Partnership (ANDP) and volunteers

Left: Vine City Neighborhood/Georgia Dome. *CODA Archive*.

Right: RDA Memorial and Square, Mechanicsville redevelopment. *Beatriz Coll; artist Emma Amos*.

constructed new homes along the Pryor Street route to the Olympic Stadium. The more fundamental changes were: 1) the establishment of community development corporations (CDCs) in several poor neighborhoods, and 2) the installation of legal and institutional infrastructure necessary to foster development in areas beyond the reach of the private sector.

The business community suspended its skepticism and mistrust of community development initiatives, and community groups set aside their reciprocal animosity, yielding new development in poor neighborhoods. Five city or metro-wide nonprofits developed the capability to augment indigenous redevelopment of poor neighborhoods. Habitat for Humanity and Charis Community Housing each constructed more than one hundred units of ownership housing during the run up to the Olympics.[*]

---

[*] Source: Keating Larry, Creighton Max, and Abercrombie, Jon. *Community Development: Building on a new Foundation*; Sjoquist, David L. et al. 1997. "The Olympic Legacy: Building on What Was Achieved." Research Atlanta Inc. School of Policy Studies, Georgia State University.

PUBLIC PARKS

The Olympics provided an opportunity to expand Atlanta's public green space considerably. Several smaller parks were located within the borders of the Olympic Ring, and three major ones lie just outside its east perimeter. Centennial Olympic Park, inside the ring and thus part of CODA's public spaces program, is the prime example of Olympic-era transformation, but the larger parks on the edge of the Olympic ring—Freedom, Piedmont and Grant—also benefited from significant private and nonprofit investments at the time. Investments to parks in the Olympic Ring during the Olympic period are shown in Table 2 in the appendix.

Freedom Park

Freedom Park was the largest new urban park built in the United States in the second half of the twentieth century. It was cobbled out of the rights-of-way of two proposed freeway connections dating from the late 1960s. All of the homes were demolished when work stopped, but not the trees. Based on an initial idea from landscape architect Jim Wylie, Mayor Jackson asked his COO, Jules Sugarman, to oversee an official concept plan for the city in 1973, which was prepared by architect Randal Roark, then of Arkhora Associates. A coalition of neighborhoods surrounding the right of way strongly advocated for the park and for appropriate minimal infill housing on the neighborhood edges damaged by the acquisition. This coalition provided a strong east side nucleus for the neighborhood movement that was forming around what would later become the Olympic Ring. The movement had found its voice through the City's Neighborhood Planning Unit ordinance, created during this time by the city's commissioner of planning, Leon Eplan. Land was acquired in the center of the right of way for the Carter Presidential Library, which was built on this site in the 1980s. Then, after a protracted battle with the city and adjacent neighborhoods, the Georgia DOT finally returned the land to the city in the early '90s, along with an agreement to build a smaller parkway around the library. CODA managed both the master planning process and the first phase of construction valued at $1 million, funded by a grant from the Woodruff Foundation in time for the Olympics. The park contains 210 acres exclusive of the parkway and the Carter Library. The Freedom Park Conservancy was formed in 1997 and has managed development from that time.

Piedmont Park

Piedmont Park was designed by the famed Olmsted brothers on the site of the 1893 Cotton States Exposition and has served as the city's signature green space since. Thanks to the formation of the public-private Piedmont Park Conservancy in 1990, a master plan was approved, and a visitor's center was renovated in time for the Olympics. Renovation and expansion have been extensive in the post-Olympic period.

Grant Park

Grant Park, the oldest in the city, is home to the Atlanta Zoo and housed the Cyclorama, a diorama depicting the Battle of Atlanta in the Civil War. It is also the terminus of the Georgia Avenue Olympic Pedestrian Corridor. A master plan was commissioned in 1996, the Grant Park Conservancy was formed and its restoration has proceeded in the post-Olympic period.

Downtown Parks

- The signature public space built for the Olympics is Centennial Olympic Park, which has been previously described. It added twenty acres of parkland to the city's core.
- Woodruff Park, built in 1973 at the city's historic Five Points intersection, was completely rebuilt for the Olympics for $6 million. After the games, Georgia State assumed the responsibility for maintenance, and Woodruff Park became a central green space for the downtown campus.
- John Wesley Dobbs Plaza was created along Auburn Avenue, honoring the unofficial mayor of the Sweet Auburn historic district.
- Two specialty parks, the Folk Art Park and De-Code Re-code Atlanta Plaza, were integrated with public art installations by winners of the "Public Space in the New American City" open competition, jointly sponsored by CODA and the Architecture Society of Atlanta.
- Four smaller parks and/or plazas along some of the pedestrian corridors, including Hardy Ivy Park and Spring Walton Park.

Significant Supporting Investments

Many investments in the region's overall infrastructure have not made the inventory of direct contributions to the Olympics per se but substantially contributed to support of the Games and to permanent long-term improvement of Atlanta. These include:

MARTA and GDOT

MARTA (Metropolitan Atlanta Rapid Transit Authority) added three rail stations and seven miles of track to meet Olympic demand. The trains ran twenty-four hours a day, the cost of which was negotiated with ACOG, and travel was free to anyone with an event ticket. Managing this complex system required 15,415 paid staff and 6,000 volunteers. GDOT (Georgia Department of Transportation) used federal funds to create an intelligent transportation system to manage and monitor the existing and anticipated traffic demand, especially on Atlanta's expansive freeways.

> *In addition, the federal government provided about $114 million so that three transit projects in Atlanta would be completed in time for the 1996 Olympics Games. The three transit projects were the North Line Rail Extension, the Atlanta University Center Pedestrian Walkway, and the Metropolitan Atlanta Regional Transit Authority Intelligent Transportation System. Specifically, DOT provided approximately $17 million to state and local transit and transit planning agencies to pay for the delivery, operation, and return of the 1,500 buses, which were borrowed from communities throughout the United States. These buses were used as the principal transportation system for Olympic spectators and Paralympics athletes. The local transit agencies allocated and used about $11 million for the regular Olympic Games and about $6 million for the Paralympics Games.**

Hartsfield-Jackson International Airport

Though Hartsfield International was already the second-busiest airport in the country, the City of Atlanta issued bonds of $350 million in 1991

---

* The Atlanta Committee for the Olympic Games. *The Official Report of the Centennial Games.* Atlanta: Peachtree Press, 1997.

to build a dedicated international concourse, which opened in 1994. This expanded capacity for international traffic, created an efficient destination for international flights and established Atlanta as a major international transportation hub. The city also undertook a $250 million program of passenger improvements, including a new atrium, designed by African American architect Oscar Harris and opened in 1996 in time for the Olympics. Atlanta's airport became the world's busiest in 1998, and the growth in international passengers created demand for an independent international terminal, which was opened in 2012. This terminal was part of a larger program of capital improvements that included, among other things, a fifth runway, new control tower and state-of-the-art baggage-handling system—it all cost about $9 billion, nearly four times the 1996 Olympics.

Georgia Power

Georgia Power and its parent, Southern Company, took a broad approach to their investment in the Games. In addition to the public responsibility of providing a secure working power grid, there were three initiatives:

- Make direct infrastructure enhancements, specifically including adequate nighttime lighting for events and corridors.
- Ensure that all communities involved realized a direct community benefit.
- Provide long-term infrastructure for future economic development in the state.

Georgia Power's direct contributions to the Olympics included special street lighting and venue lighting, investment in the torch tour and innovative bus technology with both electric and zero-emissions technology. It set up separate, temporary power systems for the Opening and Closing Ceremonies with 100 percent redundancy and for the World Congress Center press and security venue with 200 percent redundancy. In addition, electrical power to Games venues required a $67 million investment to bring the existing downtown grid to full capacity; then, an additional, temporary 100 percent was added to serve the Olympic Ring area during the games. The Georgia Power Olympics projects were implemented under the strong leadership of Olympics Coordinator Kay B. Lee and CEO Alan Franklin.

Operation Legacy

This partnership created by the private power utility Georgia Power with support from NationsBank, the Georgia Department of Industry, Trade and Tourism; the Governor's Economic Development Council; the Georgia Chamber of Commerce and the Metro Atlanta Chamber of Commerce to utilize the Olympics as a marketing tool for industrial recruitment and economic development. Operation Legacy targeted emerging industries such as telecommunications, technology and a broadly defined sports-and-entertainment industry, with the idea that these industries would respond favorably to the benefits of Atlanta's Olympic Games exposure as well as to the "bricks and mortar" by-products of the Games, for example, fiber optic cable and other technology left behind in the media headquarters and sports facilities. One year after the Games, Operation Legacy had generated more than 2000 new jobs and by the end of the third year, it had exceeded its goal of 6000 new jobs.[*]

The Paralympics

The Paralympic Games is a major international multi-sport event involving athletes with a range of physical disabilities, governed by an International Paralympic Committee separate from but allied with the IOC. Started in 1948, the Paralympics has, since 1988, been scheduled two or three weeks after the Olympic Games in the same host city and using the same venues. Since 1992, this event has consistently drawn more than 3,000 athletes from at least 100 nations. The Atlanta Paralympics was held on August 16–25, 1996, with 3,259 athletes from 104 nations. The event cost $81 million and was the first to get mass-media sponsorship. In all, about 4,500 people attended, and there were 2,088 media representatives present. The Olympic Village housed its athletes and coaches.

---

[*] Engle, Sam Marie. "The Olympic Legacy in Atlanta," *University of New South Wales Law Journal* 22, no. 3 (1999): 902.

FUNDING THE GAMES

Funding the ACOG Improvements

Presented here are ACOG's expenditures and revenues, per the official post-Olympics report. The sources of these funds and other contributions to the Games are shown in Table 3 in the appendix. In documents issued by ACOG, the point is consistently made that the Atlanta Olympics was entirely privately funded. This assertion does not consider, however, that ACOG received substantial funding from many federal sources, nor does it consider projects external to ACOG, which had many sources of funds, both public and private, including the City of Atlanta and CODA. It also does not consider the nearly $1 billion other entities spent in preparation for the Games. Many of these projects may have been completed after the Olympics, but they were necessary in preparing the city for the Games and were scheduled accordingly. These are shown in Table 8 and also Table 7 in the appendix.

Funding the CODA Improvements

The total expenditure for CODA's permanent improvements in preparation for the Olympics was $75 million. Tables 4 and 5 in the appendix detail these expenditures. Table 8 shows costs for the 1996 Olympics by all sources of funds across major contributing entities. This includes both Olympic venues and capital improvements to prepare the City for the Games.

CODA drew primarily on the federal Transportation Enhancement Activities (TEA) program legislation in 1991 for funding most of the main pedestrian corridors. Other corridors were funded by several other federal programs (bringing the total expenditure of federal funds to about $24.7 million) and the 1994 local bond referendum (with other local public sources totaling about $32.6 million). The Woodruff Foundation, along with a private funding campaign for CODA and other private and foundation funds, raised another $17.5 million. Table 4 in the appendix details the costs of the public spaces program. About 14 percent of the total funds went to four independent public parks and plaza projects while the other parks and plazas and all public artworks were included within the pedestrian corridors and other infrastructure projects. While the original fundraising target for the Coda Master Plan in 1993 was set at $121 million, by the time the Olympics opened, CODA had raised $75 million and implemented all the projects on time and within that budget.

As previously stated, the Olympic Ring neighborhoods received half of CODA's total infrastructure investment of $76 million. Other funding sources supported modest scale housing development totaling 1,317 new and rehabilitated units in these neighborhoods by 1996. CODA's approach to the neighborhoods was to establish a framework for redevelopment that could last well beyond the Olympics. Because of the short time available to implement projects and because the funds available to CODA were primarily for public improvements, actual housing and commercial development would be left to other public and private entities. Table 5 in the appendix shows the investment in CODA neighborhoods from both public and private sources totaling $87,780 million. The neighborhood development framework initiatives and results included:

- Legally adopted development plans for the five neighborhoods adjacent to Olympic venues, built on substantial community involvement;
- neighborhood sidewalks, often where there weren't any, funded from the 1994 City bond referendum for approximately $8.0 million;
- the extension of many of the Olympic pedestrian corridors into the development neighborhoods, often with public artworks and historic interpretive markers.

Funding by the Federal Government

It is often assumed the federal government does not participate directly in paying any of the Olympic costs for any U.S. city chosen to host the Games. However, a federal audit completed by the Government Accounting Office (GAO) in 2006, covering the Summer Olympics in Los Angeles in 1984, the Summer Olympics in Atlanta in 1996 and the Salt Lake City Winter Olympics in 2002, shows substantial participation by numerous federal agencies. This support came through separate departments and programs rather than as direct support earmarked for the host city or the International Olympic Committee. For the Atlanta Games, Table 6 in the appendix from the GAO indicates participation by funding sources across twenty-four federal departments totaling $608,503,000, 30 percent of which was allocated to staffing, security and other system services and 70 percent to permanent capital improvements of many kinds, most for transportation-related projects.

Significant Other Supporting Investments

The cost of the other supporting investments discussed above are listed in Table 7 in the appendix. It indicates that the total investment from other sources was $996 million, approximately one-third of the total cost of the games as outlined in Table 8. The amounts are provided by each of the sources, and some of the totals may be approximations

Summary of Costs

Table 8 shows a summary of costs for the 1996 Olympics broken down by source of funds and across the primary local entities responsible for different components of the Games. This includes not only the costs of hosting the events but also the capital improvements required to prepare the city for the Games. This is the first comprehensive cost analysis compiled for the Games. Until now, the cost has been widely cited as $1.7 million, essentially ACOG's cost of staging the Games. In Table 8, the costs for most items are known, but some are interpolations, deduced by the author from multiple sources.

This chapter has documented, for the first time, a good approximation of the total costs for staging the Atlanta Olympic Games, consistent with providing a comprehensive understanding of the Olympic era, from its inception to its legacy. The following chapter provides a comparison of the costs and other metrics for recent host cities.

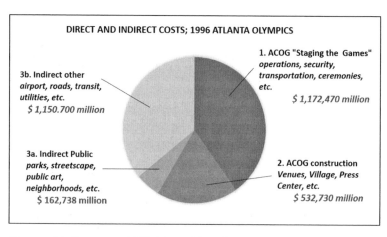

Direct and indirect costs, 1996 Atlanta Olympics.

TABLE 8

Summary of Direct and Indirect Costs for the 1996 Atlanta Centennial Olympic Games (thousands of dollars)				
Funding source	**Public: Federal**	**Public: Local/state** (including 1994 city bond referendum*)	**Private:** (Sponsors, TV rights, tickets, corporate, foundations)	**Total**
ACOG (direct)				
• Sports venues	33,650		499,080	532,730
• Other	151,350		1,021,180	1,172,470
Subtotal	$185,000		$1,520,200	$1,705,200
CODA/City				
• Public spaces	24,750	32,688	17,520	74,958
• Neighborhoods	15,000	42,916	29,864	87,780
Subtotal	$39,750	$75,604	$47,384	$162,738
Other (indirect)				
• Ga DOT	214,753			213,753
• MARTA	114,000			114,000
• Airport		**600,000		600,000
• Ga. Power		67,000		67,000
• MAOGA		100,000		100,000
• Other public	55,000			55,000
Subtotal	$383,753	$767,000		$1,150,753
TOTAL	**$608,503**	**$842,604**	**$1,567,584**	**$ 3,018,691**

*The 1994 bond referendum also included $117 million for various street, bridge and sewer projects elsewhere in the city that are not included in the table.
**A detailed breakdown of sources of airport expenditures was not available for this study but most likely included a combination of public and private sources.

Sources: CODA Archives; The Atlanta Committee for the Olympic Games. 1997. The Official Report of the Centennial Games. Atlanta: Peachtree Press. U.S. General Accounting Office. 2006. Olympic Games; Federal Government Provides Significant Funding and Support. Report to Congressional Requesters. General Accounting office. September.

CHALLENGES DURING THE GAMES

The Atlanta Olympics proved to be an event for the average American. Over 8.5 million tickets were sold, still the most for any Olympics, and unlike other Olympics, where many tickets were bought but not used, Atlanta played to a near full house. Beyond thousands of visitors from all over the world, Atlanta was more accessible to Americans in many ways; the Games were within a two-day drive by over half of the American population. The metrics addressed in chapters 4 and 5 are there for cataloguing, analyzing and interpretation. There we try to cover the most important of them. But there were also many less tangible and unspoken effects that have loomed as large as or maybe larger than the more measurable customary ones. Several of these "elephants in the room" are summarized here.

That the Games got off on the wrong foot with the media is well documented. This was primarily due to "glitches" in two systems. First, the computer system installed by IBM required 7,000 computers and 3 mainframes to cover 7,500 events across 31 venues. The system, the first to use the internet for an Olympic Games, contained never-before-used software to feed the events to the media center—and it took three days to begin functioning properly. Then, the software for the communications system, which required five thousand multilingual volunteers working on a twenty-four-hour cycle, broke down right away as a result of the overwhelming demand but was adjusted by day four. Few tend to remember that this was the first Olympics to implement this level of technological complexity. This was also the event's first use of the internet, both by the host committee and for worldwide communication. The inaugural Olympic Games website garnered up to seventeen million hits a day.

The Olympic transportation system was a mammoth undertaking, moving athletes, spectators and the Olympic family among the hotels, scattered venues and other events. This created a demand for 1,290 buses and generated a peak ridership of 14.4 million one-way riders per day. To accomplish this required the use of MARTA, on which ticketholders traveled for free, and more than 140 buses and drivers loaned by 65 different agencies from around the country. Because of Atlanta's location, many visitors came by automobile; parking spaces for 80,000 vehicles were secured on the perimeter of the city with bus connections to the venues and hotels within the Olympic Ring. In the first days, a small number of buses broke down or drivers missed routes. But this system, too, was running on all cylinders after a few days.

The "uneasy" and often tenuous private-public alliance expressed itself throughout the run-up and the execution of the Games. The business leadership's difficult relationship with the larger city showed in their steadfast opposition to the installation of public toilets on the streets of downtown Atlanta. The city had gone to great lengths to get proposals from companies producing the most technologically advanced units at the time, which would have been free if advertising were allowed on the unit. But the business leadership succeeded in scuttling the city's sustained effort to achieve what could have resulted in a lasting and high-quality response to a public necessity. Instead, "porta-potties" filled the need. Similarly, opposition surfaced to any permanent vending of food in public places. These legal issues might have been resolved had the relationships been different and the city more mature as an urban environment. Instead, the business leadership resisted progressive solutions to urban issues, because of perceptions about "undesirable" persons and concerns about their visible loitering on the street. These attitudes reflect Atlanta's larger issues of historically devaluing public space in general in favor of spaces and activities within the confines of private developments that are more easily maintained and secured.

In this context, it was astonishing that ACOG proposed the construction of Centennial Olympic Park as a central gathering place during the Games and beyond. The park was to be completely open to the public, which countered the trend of containing gathering spaces within the confines of heavily secured Olympic zones.

This commitment to open access was tarnished on day 10 of the Games. A pipe bomb was detonated from an abandoned backpack in the park, killing a visitor and a journalist (from a heart attack) and injuring 110 others. The park was open to all and did not have a security checkpoint; the bomb was detonated shortly after 1:00 a.m., when the park was at its maximum capacity. Competition continued, but the park was closed for three days while city leaders and the IOC deliberated on a proper response. It then reopened with a tribute to the victims and a celebration of the enduring human spirit. After the *Atlanta Journal and Constitution* hounded its favorite suspect, Richard Jewell, for months, the FBI concluded that he was innocent and concentrated their attention on Eric Robert Rudolph, also wanted in the bombing of an abortion clinic in Birmingham. After a years' long manhunt, the bureau finally apprehended and charged him, and the courts found him guilty of murder. Despite this tragedy, Centennial Olympic Park became the most visible iconic space of the games, a symbology that has continued to this day. The park was, and is, a great success, but the horrific bombing in the crowded park, taking two lives and injuring many others, is paradoxical given this longstanding discomfort for all public space in downtown Atlanta, fortunately now changing.

What might have been the most visible challenge to the success of the Games in Atlanta was the failed vending program. In an effort to spread the Olympic markets' benefit to the "little people," just as the big sponsors, such as Delta, Visa and Coca-Cola, were sure to do, Mayor Campbell sought to establish a street vendor program. After taking bids, the city contracted the program to a private entrepreneur in what critics called a sweetheart deal. The contractor could rent hundreds of small plots along key sidewalks, parks and plazas in the Olympic Ring and other major centers to small vendors without control of marketing or quality, shocking to both locals and visitors alike. Not only was it deemed a crass visual commercial spectacle, but the vendors complained of lack of commercial traffic and sales and most reported an economic loss as well. The contractor had projected a profit of $17 million to be shared by the city and the vendors, but in the end the contractor and the city made no more than about $2 million apiece. The result was a rash of lawsuits by vendors claiming fraud (most of which were not successful). The great irony surrounding the vending program was that, behind the beehive of activity provided by the vendor tents, the street life and support functions of a traditional urban core had all but disappeared.

Some argued that the street vending violated their notion of the spirit of the Olympics. The ironies in these critiques was the local business community and media singling out the "little guys" for trashing the city's newly upgraded multimillion streetscape environment. Without the stalls, though, the lack of street life behind the stalls may have been more desolate. The further irony in these critiques is that ACOG's sponsors' tents, huge, multicolor and logo-splashed, were deemed acceptable, even as they landed on and effectively took over many of the city's downtown park and plaza spaces.

The international and national media didn't make the same distinction between little guys and corporate giants, tarring the whole affair as tawdry marketing, some calling it the "Coca-Cola Olympics."

To protect their high-profile major sponsors, Olympic officials also complained of non-sponsor national corporations' "ambush marketing." This was a serious issue, since the Atlanta Games relied so heavily on donations from private sponsors. These accounted for 35 percent of total ACOG revenues, provided by nine "Worldwide Sponsors," ten "Centennial Olympic Partners," with limited rights to twenty-four other entities, and

Centennial Park sponsor tents. *ACOG.*

more than one hundred licenses for merchandise sales. Additionally, several sponsors paid NBC for broadcast rights. Despite the necessity of sponsor contribution to the overall revenues of this "private" Games, this very visible combination of vendors and sponsors contributed significantly to the Atlanta Games' reputation as "overly commercialized."

Perhaps more controversial was the city's approach to dealing with its homeless citizens. Estimates of the homeless ranged from six to twelve thousand living on the streets or in shelters, mostly in the core areas and in nearby neighborhoods. The city first sought to disperse the population to other places in the region, then to accommodate more in various facilities. At the same time, the offer stood for one-way bus tickets home (or elsewhere) for whoever was interested in leaving. Surely, the city could have done better, but its plight reflected the national realities borne of the 1980s federal decision to defund mental institutions, forcing thousands on to the streets or wherever. Even so, some progress was made, with more shelters provided in the "continuum of care" model, and one of the most committed providers succeeded in acquiring a building on Peachtree Street, still in use until recently, that projected a daily visible reminder of society's inequities. Less controversial but still problematic was the city's decision to expedite the code enforcement process and move to demolish some three hundred vacant and dilapidated structures, again mostly in the ring of neighborhoods surrounding the core.

4

COMPARISONS WITH OTHER OLYMPIC HOST CITIES

Olympic Financing Basics

Over the past fifty years, the Olympics have become increasingly global, with financing coming from television rights, sponsorships and ticketing, all paid for by consumers worldwide. The scale of globalization has increased since the live TV coverage of Tokyo 1964 and since internet coverage began in Atlanta 1996. This tends to make the financial management of specific Games more even and more similar.

Today, the IOC manages the revenues from TV rights, ticketing, major sponsors and licensing and official merchandise. They then make available about 50 percent of these revenues to the host Olympic Committee for the specific Games, with the rest going to the respective national committee, athletic federations (for each sport) and the IOC. This amount tends to cover the operational costs of the Games (administration, events, security and so forth). This means the cost for the construction of venues, visitor services and other support infrastructure and improvements to the city will fall on the host city and the designated Olympic Committee. With the event becoming ever larger, the need for infrastructure improvements continues to escalate, both in the development of venues and support infrastructure. These costs will increase, fall more heavily on the host city and continue to vary widely among the cities. The burden for these costs falls on a variety of public and private sources, depending on the nature of the host city and country.

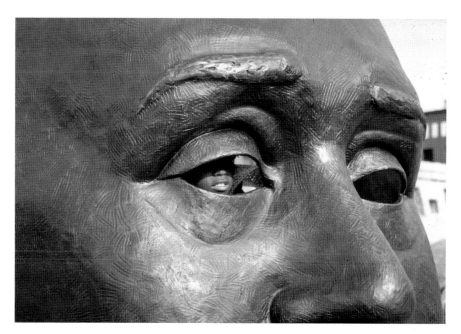

Through His Eyes, memorial to John Wesley Dobbs, civil rights leader and unofficial mayor of "Sweet Auburn." *CODA Archive, artist Ralph Helmick.*

Evaluating the performance of the Olympic Games inevitably involves comparing the host cities themselves. Each metro area offers unique history, culture, density and spatial layout among other characteristics that shape the assessment of its Games. This study emphasizes comparisons with Atlanta and finds many similarities, but it also identifies contrasts that distinguish Atlanta's 1996 Games as unique within the Olympic movement. For example, Atlanta's and Barcelona's metro areas had slightly more than two million residents in 1992, but Atlanta occupied an area twenty-six times larger. Also important is the way each city's Games is financed and how oversight is carried out, and particularly in the relationship between each city and its respective national government. Similarly, a wide gulf exists in Olympics financing. For example, Atlanta's Games were mostly privately funded, while Beijing's Games (2008) were nearly all state-financed, representing the commitment of resources for an entire nation and national culture.

The figure on page 108 summarizes the breakout of costs for the past seven Olympics in these categories and does not include Rio de Janeiro in 2016. These expenditures show wide disparities of costs, for example, indicating that Beijing spent $46.0 billion, 15.3 times more than Atlanta's total cost of $3.0

billion, adjusted for inflation. Attempting to analyze all these cost comparisons can be confusing. Most costs for a particular Olympics are expressed in U.S. dollars at the time of the Games. Some of the literature is not clear on when specific costs are incurred. For this study, when the date of the expenditures is unclear, we have assumed that it refers to the date of that Olympics. Inflation results are calculated using each country's inflation rate from the time of the Games to 2014. The resulting adjustment is shown in the figure.

This figure also summarizes the overall costs of producing the Games to the revenue source produced by ticket sales, as one way to picture the performance of the various cities. In Table 10 of the appendix, an index of total cost per ticket sold is a way to show the impact of the cost of the games when compared to the actual number of people present at the games. Although not an indicator of the overall cost and benefit of the games, both the figure on 108 and Table 10 demonstrate the extraordinary

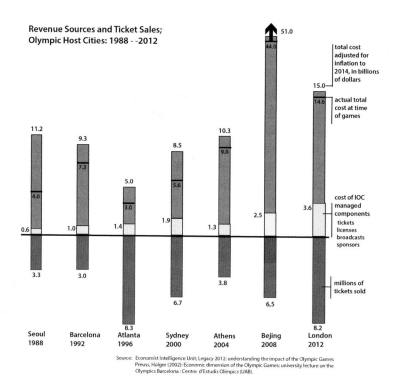

Revenue sources and ticket sales, Olympic host cities since 1988.

place of the Atlanta games compared to other host cities from 1988 through 2012. It was the Olympics with the least total cost while at the same having the most tickets sold and people in attendance. Taken together, the Atlanta Games stand out as an anomaly among other Summer Olympic Games in the past thirty-two years.

A general model has been devised by Holger Preuss for assessing costs and benefits of Olympic Games for individual host cities and is shown in Table 9 in the appendix. While specific amounts can usually be calculated for the pre-Olympic phase and the Games phase, often not all expenditures can be attributed to direct investment in Olympics events and venues, as, for example, federal expenditures for the 1996 Games. A full assessment of all investments becomes even more difficult in the post-Games phase, when it is virtually impossible to correctly identify Olympic investments and impact on the future growth and development of the host city. The initiatives and projects listed in this section were either a direct result of an investment in the Olympic Ring or were catalyzed to some degree, either to be finished by the Olympics or to be influenced by the Olympics at some time after the Games.

FINANCIAL COMPARATIVE ANALYSIS

Given the wide array of funding and operations in all the host cities, there are several main bases for comparison, including profit/loss, economic impact and public expenditures.

Profit and Loss

Each host organizing committee (for Atlanta, ACOG) usually issues a statement of profit and loss. The $3 billion cost of the Atlanta Olympics includes the $1.7 billion spent by ACOG, as described in chapter 4. Depending on the method used, analyses of the Atlanta Games have fallen between a $10 million loss and a $10 million gain, essentially resulting in a break-even condition, as predicted and concluded by ACOG. The $1.7 billion figure does not, however, consider the $1.3 billion spent by other entities. The financial balance for several host city organizing committees is shown in Table 11 in the appendix.

Economic Impact

Typically, each Olympics has an economic impact analysis prepared by one or more outside entities using a variety of conventional models. In Atlanta's case, the figure of a $5.1 billion short term impact in the state of Georgia's economy is often cited. This was a June 1995 figure prepared by Dr. Jeffery M. Humphreys and Michael K. Plummer, economics experts at the University of Georgia, using data from 1991 to 1994 and ACOG projected expenditures for 1995 to 1997. The method was a conventional one, using a three-cycle multiplier, and included direct, indirect and induced (effect of the multipliers) expenditures. The direct and indirect expenditures totaled $2.3 billion and the induced expenditures totaled $2.8 billion, creating a total impact of $5.1 billion. The results from other host cities, using a variety of methods, are indicated in Table 12 in the appendix.

Public Sector Fiscal Analysis

In "Atlanta: Race, Class and Urban Expansion" (2001), Georgia Tech planning professor Larry Keating approaches the economic impact of the Olympics as a measure of public expenditures versus public revenues at the local, state and federal levels. These are summarized in Table 13 in the appendix. It shows a total cost of $1,050.97 million and a first-year total increase in tax revenues (including federal and local income tax and sales tax) of $383.1 million, resulting in a shortfall of $668 million for the target year of 1996. However, if one makes modest assumptions on how much of the annual income tax revenues would remain at the increased level in subsequent years, it would not take but a few years for the revenues to cover the costs.

EXPANDED AGENDAS

Host cities have had to undertake (often massive) infrastructure improvements to support the Games, including transit, roadways and pedestrian and public space enhancements, permanent investments meant to stand as a continuing legacy to the Games. Two of the cities in this study, Atlanta and London, also included an aggressive program of urban community improvements focused on housing and support facilities.

Atlanta has been documented in this study to leverage the impact of the Games, particularly in the mostly lower-income neighborhoods Downtown near the Olympic venues. The amount of investment anticipated for these areas fell far short of the original plan but did set in place the political infrastructure and new public entities needed to continue this redevelopment. The other host city, London, has undertaken an ambitious program of new development in the eastern dockland along the Thames River, where the central venue and gathering space was also located. It has been described as follows:

> *Perhaps one of the most important features of the Atlanta Olympic legacy is what each host city replicated and avoided. The London Olympics provide a good model for the process.*
>
> *There, the six Host Boroughs where the Olympics were staged were able to oblige the London Committee for the Olympic Games and their delivery authority to set goals for hiring local residents and unemployed people and for procuring local businesses to provide services.*
>
> *They started with a "Creating Wealth and Reducing Poverty" action plan. They followed up with a collaboration between the delivery team, their contractors, job training providers, and community representatives to broker the process and implement the plan. Over 20 per cent of the Olympics construction and operations workforce were "locals," over 20 percent of procurement went to local businesses, and the process continues into the post-Games era.*[*]

---

[*] Conversation with Stuart Acuff. See also Gavin Poynter and Valerie Viehoff, *Mega-event Cities: Urban Legacies of Global Sports Events* (Routledge 2018).

THE ANOMALOUS OLYMPICS:
A LEGACY OF "SMALL BALL"

Even among markedly different profiles of most recent host cities, the Atlanta Olympics has proven to be an anomaly in the following ways:

1. Significantly less total cost and a break-even profit/loss statement, with two-thirds of the costs incurred by the private sector.
2. Construction and operation without national government direction or control (typical of other U.S. host cities) but with participation of twenty-four separate federal agencies making contributions across the board in operations and development.
3. Most tickets sold, equal to that of the larger 2012 London Olympics, but with more visitors actually at the events in a city that could be accessed by automobile by much of America's population.
4. A more dispersed layout, primarily using existing venues and built nearly all within the downtown
5. The lack of a spectacular architectural monument from the Olympic Games even though many such monuments are today standing empty from nearly all Olympic Cities since at least 1960. But here, after the tents folded and the smoke cleared, the icon left behind was perhaps the biggest anomaly, a new urban public space, Centennial Park, filling a void in the center of the city, a negative-space anti-architecture monument. Today visited by millions, it has brought life back to downtown and influenced much development around it.

With the advantage of hindsight, the Atlanta Olympics was an unusual event with over six million people, mostly average Americans, jostling about between dispersed venues on the downtown streets of a multiracial southern American city coping with the problems of urban America in the 1990s. The myriad accessible multicultural events of the cultural Olympiad existed alongside the hundreds of small vendor tents lining the streets ("a tawdry spectacle"). The program was meant to give the "little guy" a small piece of the commercial pie alongside the big (some would say also tawdry) sponsor tents in Centennial Olympic Park, a wide-open public space teeming with rowdy day and night activity for anyone with or without a ticket (and a ripe target for terrorism). It was a spectacle more reminiscent of a large state urban fair in middle America than a highbrow international sporting event envisioned by the Eurocentric elites who governed the IOC. All of this most likely contributed to the IOC's condescending (and some would say slightly racist) evaluation of the Atlanta Games not being the "best Olympics ever." Nevertheless, a kind of "peoples' Olympics" emerged somewhat unwittingly in stark contrast to the prevailing IOC model.

Taken together, these anomalies have often been the source of criticism of Atlanta Games with media tags like "The no frills, no thrills Olympics" and a "missed opportunity." But in retrospect, ACOG played the hand it was dealt of dispersed venues in a difficult urban environment with lasting success, and CODA adopted a positive strategy out of many small improvements and interventions still serving as points of connection and leverage throughout downtown and the adjacent neighborhoods. Together, this anomalous "small ball" Olympics has left behind many catalytic investments that have had a kind of time-released positive effect on the city around it and possibly could be seen as a model for more sustainable Olympic Games in the future.

The long-term effects of this dynamic "concoction" are discussed in chapter 5.

5

THE LEGACIES

Introduction

The Centennial Olympic Games concluded on August 4, 1996. In his closing assessment, Juan Antonio Samaranch, president of the International Olympic Committee, declared them the "most exceptional" Games ever. This pronouncement varied significantly from the traditional "best Games ever" accolade that had concluded previous Games. For close readers of protocol, this characterization was deemed at best a lukewarm judgment. The tepid endorsement, beyond the tragic bomb episode, reflected a number of bothersome anomalies for the IOC, particularly its lack of dominance in the decision-making processes and its less-than-expected profit from the Games.

As reported in earlier chapters, the Atlanta Games themselves were a great popular success, drawing greater audiences at more affordable costs than any Olympics before or since. In addition, unlike many host cities, the principal sponsor, ACOG, made a profit, and the city came out debt-free. ACOG's reasoned decision to locate most of the venues in Atlanta's downtown's languishing core proved to be a brilliant choice. Serendipitously, the Olympic investments coincided with changes toward urbanizing markets. The magnitude, timing and quality of the public infrastructure framework built to host the Games responded to these new markets. They showed promise in places where hope for years had not been evident and where grit had dominated.

Fountain of Rings in Centennial Olympic park. *CODA Archive.*

In spite of these accomplishments, or perhaps because the magnitude of their impact had not yet sunk in, for several weeks after the Games closed, a sort of pall hung over the city, a letdown and anxiety about what to do next. The local media (at least the mainstream outlets) at once rehashed what they viewed as the negatives, as evidenced by an *Atlanta Journal* headline of the time, "Downtown Boosters Coping with Post-Olympic Letdown." Others worried that the event might just be a blip in what they viewed as the city's ongoing decline, a last hurrah in a thirty-year slide from 500,000 to 400,000 people. This reporting reflected business leaders' frustration with the ways of city governance generally and concern that the government was ill-prepared to move forward on the momentum the Olympics had generated. And it's true that not much was on the drawing boards right at that moment. It should be noted, too, that the white media and the mayor, Bill Campbell, by this time had developed an unhelpful hate-hate relationship.

To frame a report and an assessment about the event's legacy, then, it is important to understand the complex, messy and uneasy organizational interrelationships that somehow succeeded in delivering the Games.

115

The intense building and then sustaining activity that spanned the '90s and onward is infused with a complex range of problems, choices and outcomes. Further, the city's major development actors perceived the Olympics decade of the '90s through different lenses, with each responding accordingly. Their disparate realities spanned ACOG, the private sector, the city government and the affected communities, all interwoven with economic and real estate markets and the media. While there was some improvement, longstanding culturally and historically driven attitudes pervaded the process. The mainly white private sector players telegraphed some scorn for the Black-run government, whose leaders likewise signaled a certain hostility and undertow of distrust, borne of an experience of broken promises and inequitable distribution of the public's resources. Each had some say in deciding how plans, projects, priorities, funding and responsibilities would go down, but the final say was elusive. The uneasiness reflected in their discomfort with having to work so closely together was a unique experience for many. The hard deadline pushed aside historic disagreements, cross-purposes, white-Black and private-public animosities, at least for the moment.

The organizational model that evolved to deliver the Games mirrored these complexities. It was generally more inclusive and diffuse than the unified authority used by most host cities up to that time. Indeed, after its Atlanta experience the IOC insisted on such authorities being in place to exercise overall control of all aspects of the Games.

The Atlanta model's messy structure reflected the diverse range of interests and perspectives already identified. Given its complexity, the evolving delivery structure was more transparent and interactive than a top-down organization would have permitted, reflecting the inclusive richness of a broader public. Perhaps more important, people with little in common, who may have never even met, had to listen to one another across the chasms of race and class.

Whatever else might come, the Games themselves had to go on; all of the construction, the delivery logistics, the money, the approvals and the security infrastructure had to be in place—period. As a result, putting on the Games had a catalyzing effect. Projects that had been talked about for years suddenly got a boost. And projects that hadn't been dreamed of cropped up and got done, or at least got started. Others fell by the wayside. The effect of the deadline served to accelerate bogged-down, long-standing projects, and the focusing moment prompted rethinking of old problems and discovery of new approaches and opportunities.

Guiding the course of these development initiatives were significant policy shifts aimed to catalyze Mayor Jackson's and then Mayor Campbell's commitment to take advantage of the Olympic moment to recast the city's future, to reverse its long, slow decline and to seek ways to meet needs of long-neglected populations. Supporting these shifts was a commitment to support comprehensive and thoroughgoing city planning at all levels as the connective thread for framing the city's investment and regulatory priorities.

After two earlier bond financing attempts had failed, awareness of the Olympic opportunity and recognition of its urgency built enough confidence among the citizenry to vote in favor of a $150 million bond issue in 1994. The proceeds were committed to addressing a panoply of citywide deferred maintenance items, including streets, sidewalks, bridges, sewers, storm drainage and parks improvements. Altogether, the success of the initiative signaled the will of the citizenry to tax themselves to improve conditions citywide. Many of the bond projects were under construction toward the end of the Olympic run-up; others were completed over the next several years (see chapter 3 for details). The program served to make inroads into remedying neglect, responding to neighborhood need and priorities and upgrading infrastructure to attract new private investment.

The intense activities called for extraordinary efforts from Mayor Campbell and his staff to navigate the twists and turns that always dog the city's review, approval and implementation processes. COO Byron Marshall, Chief of Staff Steve Labovitz, Deputy Chief of Staff Sharon Gay and Olympics Coordinator Susan Pease Langford somehow figured out how to get a somewhat rambunctious city council and all the city's departments to deliver what they absolutely had to deliver at the end of the day.

Such, then, was the organizational setting when the Games closed, posing these big questions: Would the parties who had come together to plan for and pull off the event be able to sustain collaborative relationships to build the city going forward? Or would they revert to pre-Olympic positions, where uncoordinated one-off developer-driven projects would pop up by whatever means it took to get them going?

Researchers assessing the ultimate impact of hosting the Olympic Games have posited a reasonably succinct framework for evaluating their legacy, which provides a basis for measuring the Atlanta's experience.[*] In addition to the quantifiable legacy investments described in earlier

---

[*] Engle, 1999; Andranovich, Burbank and Heying, 2001.

chapters, the following questions frame the less-quantifiable, long-term legacies of Atlanta's Games:

- Did the Games leave behind buildings, monuments or public spaces that have ongoing functional and/or iconic value?
- Did the Games create traditional forms of economic impact in the near and long term?
- Did the Games raise the international visibility and business opportunities for the Atlanta city and region?
- Did the Games incent or influence investments to raise the social capital for improving the city's quality of life?
- Did the Games create momentum for a change in the way we think about and invest in the center city?

To these measures, in the Atlanta context, we might simply add this question: "On balance, did the Games leave Atlanta better off than it was before?" The short answer to all these questions is "yes." The longer answer includes qualifiers and caveats: the content of this chapter.

CITY POLICY SHIFTS

The Renaissance Policy Board

As the Olympics were winding down, Mayor Campbell's staff, led by Chief Operating Officer Byron Marshall along with citizen leadership, embraced a post-Games strategy conceived by CODA's president Clara Axam and consultant David Crane. Mid-1996, the staff induced him to convene what came to be known as the Atlanta Renaissance Program policy group to answer the question what next? The group, chaired by Roberto Goizueta, CEO of Coca-Cola, was composed of eighteen top-level business and civic leaders, staffed by Marshal and Planning Commissioner Mike Dobbins for the city, Randy Roark for CODA and Dr. David Sjoquist for Georgia State University's research arm. McKinsey and Company lent pro bono support to the group. Its purpose, using the impetus of the Olympics, was to think through the city's current condition, compare that with peer cities, analyze its options and suggest measures to implement what the group hoped might propel

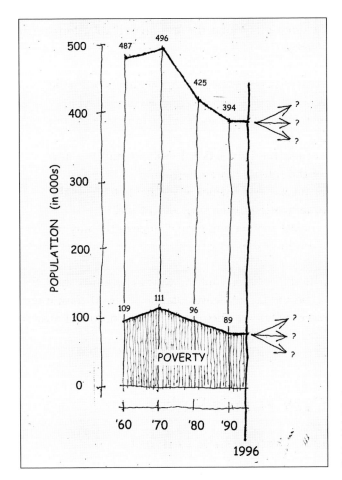

Whither next? Population and poverty trajectory, up to 1996, showing range of possible trend futures. *Mike Dobbins.*

the city along a path back from its thirty-year decline toward a unifying and positive vision for the future.

McKinsey compared Atlanta with other cities of similar size and demographic make-up across a comprehensive range of condition indicators, factors and trends. At the time, Detroit was deemed to more closely resemble Atlanta than the other peer cities chosen.

From its problem definition, analysis and recommendations, the report focused on the factors that had been contributing to Atlanta's pervasive poverty, job and population stagnation, infrastructure deficiencies and development and investment obstacles. The finding that seemed most focusing and thus gained the most traction could be boiled down into a simple one-liner: get more middle-income people to move into the city. The consultant's focus on shifting the demographic make-up of the city tracked with its analysis of other cities, where a larger middle class, a smaller lower-income component and a less sharp divide between rich and poor correlated well with healthier economies and city quality of life. The mayor, the city council, the Metro Atlanta Chamber of Commerce and other leaders endorsed the study as identifying a sound, clear and measurable way to move forward.

Policies and Programs

The city staff, then, with Roark's and Sjoquist's support, set about dealing with the "how to do it" questions, absorbing the McKinsey work into its policy thinking and the city's realistic capabilities. They sought to analyze more closely shifts that might be useful to carry the ideas forward. On that base, the city's report for moving forward, written by Dobbins and edited by Sjoquist, recommended job-generation, housing stabilization and neighborhood revitalization strategies, along with real estate investment measures and upgrades to its infrastructure. This document, then, helped to set in motion the necessary policy and program changes.

A brief rundown shows that over the next few years, the city achieved positive advances on all of these fronts. From the city's perspective, based on information in hand about demographic shifts and building permit trends, McKinsey's housing target of twenty-five thousand more middle class housing units in ten years seemed daunting in early 1997. Yet that goal was well along within seven years, signaling private sector confidence in spreading residential investment previously focused in Buckhead to long-disinvested other parts of the city. Neighborhood housing revitalization and housing initiatives were showing progress, building on CODA's redevelopment planning as described earlier. The Atlanta Housing Authority, reversing years of neglect and living in HUD's doghouse, complemented the city's success. Following up on its two Olympic time frame mixed-income project redevelopment initiatives, it extended its redevelopment agenda to all its properties, consisting of more than thirteen thousand housing units, as described later in more detail.

The business recruitment goal continued to see advancements in both Atlanta and the wider region, as described in chapter 3. Leaders in those efforts included private sector players like Georgia Power, which accelerated upgrades to its power grid, and the Metropolitan Atlanta Chamber of Commerce's focused strategies developed by its president, Sam Williams, joined by nonprofit community improvement districts and the Atlanta Development Authority.

Planning Initiatives

Side by side with policy responses to the Renaissance group's findings, the city considered the likely effects of emerging trends showing that demographics and markets were working in favor of the chances for city regeneration. Planning staff analyses suggested that shifts underway in population make-up were significant and that the city with its shifts in policy and planning initiatives was pretty well positioned to take advantage of them. A growing percentage of seniors and empty-nesters, a shrinking of families with children and a generation of young adults who grew up in suburbs but were not interested in staying, all tracked well with investing in the core city. Living closer to work, stores, services and amenities, not needing a yard, not wanting to drive as much, all could combine with a safe, pleasant and reliably improving civic environment to capture growing market share. While not a cause of nationally occurring market shifts, the city's Olympics response created the kinds of walkable, well-lit street environments, the kinds of parks, mixed-density, mixed-use developments and the dawning environmental consciousness that attracted prospective urban dwellers. It was clear that a change moment was at hand, that there was a growing demand for choice in where and how to live, work and travel. "Connecting" was a growing value among populations that grew up disconnected. The Olympic preparations fit well to jumpstart core city revitalization and redevelopment. The later success of the 1999 bond referendum validated these analyses.

The city planning department developed an aggressive agenda for inserting quality-of-place measures into regulatory and funding priorities. The department set up a strong urban design group that led much of that work, headed by Alycen Whiddon and including recent Georgia Tech grads Caleb Racicot, Aaron Fortner and Enrique Bascunana. Beverly Dockery-Ojo and Renee Kemp-Rotan provided additional staff design skills and oversight. They grounded their work in the broad policy framework emerging from the Renaissance groups' studies along with the city's yearly citizens-engaged Comprehensive Development Plan updates and through its Neighborhood Planning Unit (NPU) system.

Charlie Battle, a core member of ACOG, later as president of Central Atlanta Progress, picked up the core planning theme of connectivity and incorporated "connecting the dots" as an important consideration in CAP's strategies.

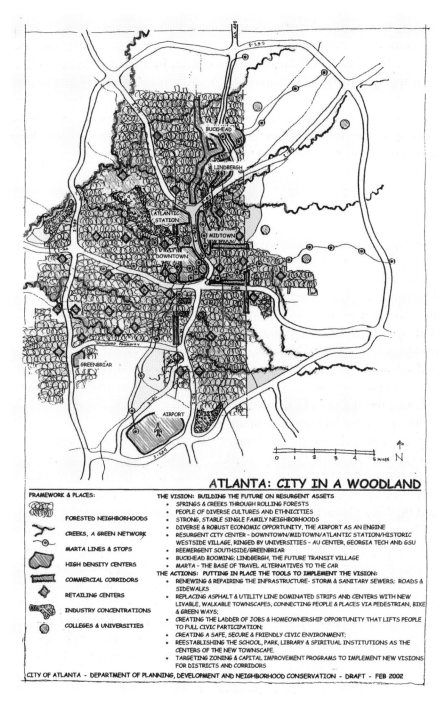

Dobbins produced one-page sketch maps that communicated the big takeaways from the three-hundred-page plus yearly Comprehensive Development Plans, this one from 2002.

To better communicate its Comprehensive Development Plan, a three-hundred-page document, Dobbins created a one-page illustration and caption that summarized the key visions coming from its extensive process of outreach to the NPUs. Then, using the yearly updated plan as a base, the city launched multiple new zoning initiatives—at parcel scale, in major districts like Downtown, Midtown and Buckhead and citywide—all incorporating form and function priorities informed by neighborhood groups, local businesses, developers, planning professionals and markets.

Zoning

The department introduced new quality-of-life classifications, encouraging or requiring mixed-use projects that would look and function better. The Multi-Family Residential, Mixed Residential Commercial, Live Work, Neighborhood Commercial and Special Public Interest districts differed in allowable density, scale and the like, but shared urban design place making characteristics. These efforts put the guidance in place to ensure that new and retrofit development would encourage mixed-use, pedestrian-friendly and parking-shielding patterns to enliven otherwise car-dominated cityscapes. For example, provisions included "build to" lines in place of parking setbacks, transparency in street fronting façades, sidewalk enhancements in widths, plantings and lighting, among others.

The staff offered these changes to each NPU for consideration, returning two or three times to make sure that comments and concerns were addressed. With ongoing guidance from Bob Zoeckler, David Blum and Lem Ward of the law department, the city's Zoning Review Board and the City Council thus unanimously adopted the package of quality-of-life zoning changes. A key feature of the department's strategy was to encourage adoption of one or another of the new categories by the emerging private development community. Their applications of the alternate rules popped up throughout the city, especially in newly hot markets on the east side of town. Recognizing that development rules are always and should be always changing in interaction with markets and cultural preferences, the follow-on strategy was to allow development under the new rules or the old rules for a time and then scuttle the old rules. Administrations and planning practices that followed, however, lost interest in this incremental approach.

Beyond the citywide zoning modifications, the department extended, sharpened and improved its Special Public Interest (SPI) zoning districts to include spatial and contextual form and flexibility provisions. The city put these districts in place initially in the 1970s under the Jackson mayoralty and Leon Eplan's first tenure as planning commissioner, primarily as a way to better shape growth around then emerging MARTA rail stations.

As a step forward in the emerging post-Olympic strategies, the city reshaped the SPI designation to improve the civic realm, to strengthen incentives and to streamline its use to attract suitable development for the changing markets. One of the streamlining provisions of the new SPI districts that exemplifies the improved city partnerships with the development community shortened the review process as compared to conventional zoning practice. SPI districts are required to put in place a development review committee that is inclusively constituted with business, city and community representation. Its purpose is to review a development proposal's compliance with the general provisions of SPI zoning and then to consider the particulars to ensure compatibility with visions and policies held by the convening agency and the city's comprehensive development plan. It then renders an advisory opinion to the city planning department, which then may approve or modify the proposal and issue a Special Administrative Permit (SAP), thus bypassing the more ponderous process required for de novo zoning processes. This process was initially put in place for Midtown, following its visioning and policy-setting Blueprints process.

Funding

Using the transformational success of the CODA projects, the city's planning capabilities prioritized the city's public improvement commitments to complement oncoming development within the new zoning guidance. To help pay for the requisite improvements to the public environment, it instituted new and redirected existing development finance tools. These included Community Improvement Districts (CID), Tax Allocation Districts (TAD), tax-deferred development incentives, ADA's bonding capacity, community development block grants, low-income housing tax credits, creative blending of public and private fund sources and more. The goal was to meet the emerging demands for urban settings that both worked well and appealed. In addition, the city and its various partners used regionally controlled funds under the Atlanta Regional Commission's (ARC) Livable

Centers Initiative (LCI) program to both plan and implement streetscape and plaza development (more about this later). In addition, city planning was an essential partner in large-scale redevelopment projects that tapped new markets for in-town living, working and shopping complexes as viable options to the suburban-dominated patterns that had characterized the region's growth.

The way the CID tool worked, enabled statewide in 1984, gave designated municipal districts the ability to self-tax for the purpose of improving their public realms. Uses of the funds includes streetscape improvements, other infrastructure enhancements, better coordinated policing, maintenance and marketing programs. The city enabled the establishment of CIDs in several business-centered districts, beginning with Central Atlanta Progress's (CAP) formation of the Atlanta Downtown Improvement District (ADID) in 1995, followed soon thereafter in Midtown and Buckhead.

Paralleling the initiation of CIDs came another planning and funding initiative whose purposes and priorities tracked the new post-Olympics visions. Tax Allocation Districts (outside of Georgia known as tax increment financing) allowed the city to devote anticipated tax gains through a development's rise in tax value to be sequestered to defray their development costs for public serving uses, like parking or streetscape improvements.

Soon after these funding and development support tools had come online, in 1999 the aforementioned ARC Livable Centers Initiative program used federal funding to advance its support for alternative transportation. The program thus funded plans to develop more compact, transit and bike/pedestrian friendly development patterns. The LCI offered planning grants to jurisdictions committed to the goal. If the plans turned into supportive regulatory measures, capital funding on a competitive basis could be available for their implementation.

In 1999, as an added boost, showing optimism in the post-Olympic process, citizens overwhelmingly approved an additional follow-up $150 million infrastructure bond issue, styled as a quality-of-life initiative. This aimed at improving streetscapes, parks, roads and sewers. These projects came up through the Neighborhood Planning Units and then councilmembers. Part of the city's approval strategy was to ensure more or less equal funding for each council district, with a bump for the core, recognizing its magnitudes of needs and intensity of activity.

Partnerships

The city used these regulatory and funding tools to support development initiatives, large and small, whose purposes tracked with Maynard Jackson's and then Mayor Campbell's follow-up commitments to establish citywide improvement programs. The city's planning department and development authority were essential partners in facilitating large-scale redevelopment projects that tapped new markets for in-town living, working and shopping complexes as viable options to the suburban-dominated patterns that had characterized the region's growth. The city sought to use its capital funding resources and development regulatory tools to try to remedy the effects of long-term disinvestment in many areas in and around the core city. Using these new tools, we describe a sampling of the partnerships and projects that marked progress in turning the city around, beginning with the Olympic Ring in the citywide context.

Picture the Olympics as a stone dropping into the quiet pond that was the downtown core at the time; the splash and then ripples spread outward to affect the core city, its neighborhoods and adjacent business concentrations. Following that order, the following sections report on the immediate CODA and ACOG legacies, the city's policy, planning, and development partnership shifts, projects that fell into the Olympic Ring and then the ripples out to the north and to the east.

CODA Legacy

Mayor Jackson established three priorities for CODA to carry out on behalf of the city leading into the Olympics:

- design and build the six primary pedestrian corridors connecting MARTA to the main Olympic venues
- supplement the Olympic agenda with community-serving public improvements
- pursue improvements to the fifteen neighborhoods surrounding downtown and the Olympic Ring

Operating in a tight time frame with a tight budget, as detailed in chapter 3, in just three years CODA was remarkably successful. So what happened to this array of initiatives, and what is CODA's legacy?

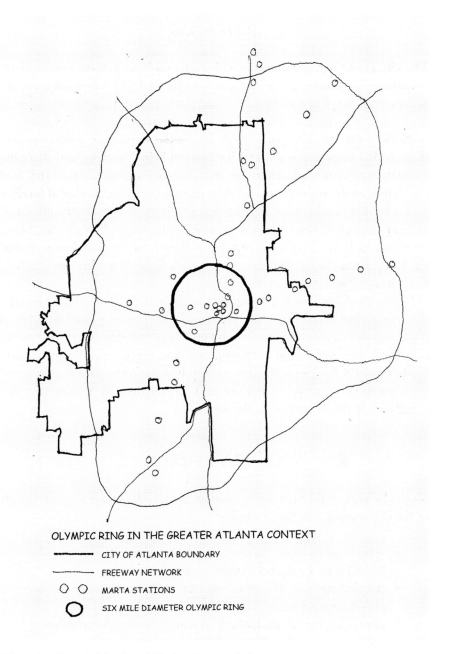

OLYMPIC RING IN THE GREATER ATLANTA CONTEXT

— CITY OF ATLANTA BOUNDARY

— FREEWAY NETWORK

◌ ◯ MARTA STATIONS

◯ SIX MILE DIAMETER OLYMPIC RING

Where the Olympic Ring fits within the city as a whole.

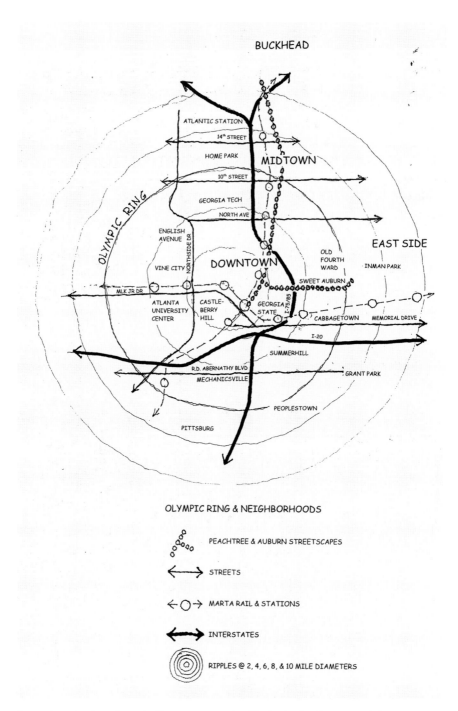

Stone dropping into the quiet Downtown pond, with ripples flowing out mainly to the north and east.

Streets

Overall, the streetscape programs have permanently changed the character of the core city, set new standards citywide for street and sidewalk design and changed the culture of what streets should be and whom they should serve. Each of these streetscape improvements have their own complications, calling on the city and state transportation agencies to rearrange their historic car-serving priorities to incorporate the full range of travel modes that citizens and then markets were beginning to demand.

With the Olympics award in 1990, Central Atlanta Progress organized a design competition in 1991 that marked the realization that Atlanta's defining streets—Peachtree and Auburn—were shabby, uninviting and not particularly functional for the range of travel types they were supposed to accommodate. The purpose was to replace the barren with the gracious, the forbidding with the inviting. The oncoming Olympics brought an urgency—and funding support—to get the work completed in time. Nimrod Long and Associates from Birmingham won the competition. With the design in hand, CODA, with city and CAP support, then directed the implementation of the Peachtree Street transformation. With comparable improvements to intersecting iconic Auburn Avenue to the east, work on the two went forth on

Auburn Avenue with Prince Hall Masons headquarters in the foreground, the center of John Wesley Dobbs's domain in historic "Sweet Auburn." *Jeb Dobbins.*

an accelerated timetable. Paralleling the work on Peachtree, CODA totally rebuilt and richly fountained Woodruff Park. Similarly, CODA's John Wesley Dobbs Plaza, honoring that civil rights icon, punctuated the Auburn Avenue improvements that linked to the Martin Luther King Jr. historic district.

Together these projects set the model and the precedent for complementary streetscape and park extensions into and through Midtown and ultimately beyond. The results thus reinforced Peachtree's historic Native American ridgeline trail as the spine of the linear city, establishing the infrastructure base necessary to attract new investment along its length. Likewise, distinguishing the legacy of Sweet Auburn with its streetscape and historic markers reinforced its cultural and historic contributions to the development of Atlanta. As with other pre-Olympics improvement projects, the deadline played a definitive role in getting these projects built.

The development of wider, well-lit and tree-lined sidewalks along both of these two iconic streets signaled the city's commitment to refocus its energies on the role of its streets in framing future development. CODA integrated park spots and miniature plazas into the work, as detailed in chapter 3. Perhaps the streets' most dramatic contribution from a citywide perspective was a clear shift in the city's travel culture. The idea that walking might be pleasurable in this car-addicted city was radical, yet catapulted pedestrian quality and serviceability into the forefront of city priorities, now seen in an unending succession of sidewalk improvement initiatives throughout the city.

Parks and Plazas

Similarly, CODA's park and plaza work, as detailed in chapter 3, was at the nexus of lifting the city's consciousness and commitment to treasure the parks it had and stoking the desire for more and better, which has become a driving force in rebalancing capital priorities toward green space. The Olympics moment helped bring to a head the long-simmering, community-driven struggle to stop GDOT's plan to build the Stone Mountain Freeway, which was to run from downtown through settled, stable neighborhoods to Stone Mountain, eighteen miles to the east. To stop the proposed limited-access divided highway, which had the backing of both former president Jimmy Carter and former mayor Andrew Young, was a tall order. Yet effective and long-haul community organizing, led by Cathy Bradshaw, Ruth Wall, Al Caproni and many others, together with gradual changes in highway engineering attitudes toward city-rending freeways and a change

Freedom Park, now John Lewis Parkway, the city's first venture into providing trails for bikers, joggers and walkers. *Jeb Dobbins*.

in leadership at GDOT, resulted in the community's victory. Court-ordered mediation brought forth the new Freedom Park, first called "Great Park." The city was then able to negotiate a smaller parkway around the newly built Carter Library and Center on the property dubbed Freedom Parkway. The planning firm EDAW Inc. was selected to design the parkland in 1993. The city called in CODA to manage the implementation process. CODA succeeded in getting the first phases of the park in place in time for the Olympics, a feat that surely would have lagged without that deadline.

This whole story is a remarkable tribute to the importance of citizens' action to prevent a top-down, poorly thought out "solution" to a nonproblem in the face of huge political and institutional momentum. The communities that would have been ripped by the project instead achieved not just stabilization but cross-neighborhood solidarity and lasting standing to play a core role in proposals affecting their futures.

Since completed, the park has served the flanking neighborhoods with walking, jogging and biking amenities through parklands that the state had purchased for freeway right-of-way. Freedom Park thus was the east–west trail precursor of the intersecting north–south BeltLine trail, built more than ten years later.

In the same vein, the Piedmont Park Conservancy, which formed in 1991 to bring more hands-on citizens-guided resources to that park's development and management, used the Olympics attention to step up its game. With CODA's and Roark's personal support, it succeeded in getting the Piedmont Park historic visitors' center rehabbed in time for the Olympics. The level of sustained commitment by the Conservancy led to an Atlanta Regional Commission LCI grant to appropriately dress up the park's Piedmont Avenue frontages, one of its many successive additions and improvements. These initiatives signaled a rise in citizens' taking more active and focused roles in asserting their values in parks as public resources, initiatives that soon followed with the formation of the Freedom Park and the Grant Park Conservancies.

BeltLine Precursors

Still another CODA initiative, working with community developer Starling Sutton, proposed to build an electric shuttle bus service along the downtown rail corridor to connect cultural and tourist venues into the core. With the support of the cultural venues and the participation of Georgia Power and transit planner Manuel Padron, CODA undertook a feasibility study to determine whether the path, by now called the Cultural Shuttle, could be designed though a combination of city streets and the still active freight rail corridor, to serve Olympics visitors. Unfortunately, though, the results concluded that experimental zero-emissions bus technology was not advanced enough to serve this ring corridor in time for the Olympics.

In the same time frame, the idea of using underutilized tracks as a rails-to-trails amenity was burbling along in the city planning department during Eplan's tenure. Staff planner Alycen Whiddon and the trail-building PATH Foundation leader, Ed McBrayer, were working on the broader loop that was ultimately to become a large portion of the BeltLine. Their work became a prominent part of the city's Parks, Open Space and Greenway Trails Plan, adopted into the city's Comprehensive Development Plan in 1993. The concept sustained its support into the post-Olympic period, with the help of a master's thesis six years later by Georgia Tech city planning and architecture student Ryan Gravel, a project whose trajectory is described more fully later.

Carnegie Pavilion on Peachtree Street, now a landmark and backdrop for thousands of visitors' photos and selfies. *Jeb Dobbins.*

Public Art

As detailed in chapter 3, a co-implementer with ACOG of the Cultural Olympiad, CODA carried out twenty-four public art installations, all intended as permanent installations that continue to mark key public places throughout downtown. Upkeep of these parts of the legacy were a concern, but fortunately, led by the Atlanta Public Art Legacy Fund (see below), with strong support by Jennifer Ball of Central Atlanta Progress, Robert Witherspoon of the City's Office of Cultural Affairs and Lisa Cremin of the Community Foundation of Great Atlanta, most of the works have been maintained and conserved. One of these, the Carnegie Pavilion, marks the entrance to Hardy-Ivy Park, which had replaced the intersection of Peachtree and West Peachtree Streets. Its plaza has become a favorite site for tourists' photos and selfies, as well as the venue for any number of festivals, of which most enchanting is the annual Dragon Con convention.

The Atlanta Public Arts Legacy Fund

In a separate legacy initiative at the end of the Games, CODA established the Atlanta Public Arts Legacy Fund (APAL). CODA established this endowment fund as a donor-advised fund at the Community Foundation for Greater Atlanta. It was made up from several contingency accounts from various CODA public artworks projects. The fund, APAL, is dedicated to the conservation and maintenance of CODA's public artworks and to public arts awareness and stewardship citywide. It is organized as a donor-advised fund at the Community Foundation of Greater Atlanta managed by the Foundation and former CODA president, Clara Axam. APAL has relied on both the endowment and on one-time project grants to carry out its conservation work on an annual basis. CODA's Axam and Roark managed the fund, with the work itself directed by Patricia Kerlin, who had been CODA's public art projects' manager. The APAL Fund continues to be housed at the Community Foundation working in collaboration with the City to care for the Olympic art. The city's own conservation function became fully established under Camille Love, the director of the Bureau of Cultural Affairs.

The CODA Neighborhoods and the Empowerment Zone

As described in chapter 3, CODA's planning work set the stage for significant revitalization work in its priority neighborhoods and created a model for the city's follow-up planning in its 32 Empowerment Zone neighborhoods. Along with CODA's work and the Atlanta Neighborhood Development Partnership's efforts as an intermediary between the well-intended established civic organizations and grassroots-driven groups, there emerged the Atlanta Housing Association of Neighborhood-based Developers (AHAND), led by Andy Schneggenburger and Kate Little. This group sought to link the Olympic Ring neighborhood-based Community Development Corporations into a connected force for advancing their interests.

Old Fourth Ward

One of the CDCs, the Historic District Development Corporation, founded in 1980, created guiding principles to ensure that the development process responded to values held in the Old Fourth Ward neighborhood for decades. Included in those principles was a strong statement regarding non-displacement of existing residents, the preservation of the neighborhood's character and redevelopment that would restore the neighborhood as mixed income. Since the early 1990s, under the leadership of Mtamanika Youngblood, HDDC had been using a block-by-block development strategy, building new homes on vacant lots on the same streets where it had rehabbed existing dilapidated structures. In the late 1990s and into the 2000s, HDDC began developing larger multifamily and mixed-use developments in strategic locations to spark redevelopment throughout the neighborhood. Since its inception, HDDC has constructed dozens of affordable single-family, duplex and multifamily rental units around the Martin Luther King Jr. Historic District.

In another bold venture, HDDC undertook a major complicated project at the east edge of the Old Fourth Ward neighborhood that came to be known as Studioplex. Like similar loft conversions underway in Castleberry Hill, Studioplex created loft living, co-working and community serving businesses. Complicated both by unproven markets and technical and financial obstacles, HDDC partnered with a seasoned, skilled and committed development corporation, Columbia Residential, whose leader, Noel Khalil, was a veteran developer of senior housing and Low Income Housing Tax

Old Fourth Ward: Studioplex, an early venture into repurposing industrial buildings into mixed-use, neighborhood-integrated live-work opportunities. *Jeb Dobbins.*

Credit projects. This kind of partnership, while complicated by somewhat diverging interests, brought together implementation know-how with the local trust engendered by community-serving CDCs to get the job done in a way that responded to community need.

Despite best intentions and impressive achievements, however, the forces of dislocation and gentrification have crept over the neighborhood. The incremental spread, though, has allowed the neighborhood residents more time to adjust than in neighborhoods that were unprepared for a more sudden run-up of speculation and tax increases.

Peoplestown

The Peoplestown neighborhood formed its CDC as the Peoplestown Revitalization Corporation (PRC) in 1989. The PRC was chaired by Columbus Ward, who was also the president of the Peoplestown neighborhood association. The PRC benefitted from its partnership with a Community Design Center that Larry Keating, a Georgia Tech planning faculty member, established with Max Creighton as its manager. With a boost from a CODA redevelopment plan, the city supported the effort for many years through the federally funded Community Development Block Grant program. In the Olympic era, William McFarland directed the PRC, which, like others in the Olympic Ring neighborhoods, succeeded in producing housing developments that served below-market renter markets, signaling changes to come in the neighborhoods.

Mechanicsville

CODA prepared the redevelopment plan for the Mechanicsville neighborhood, west of the stadium. Working with CODA, ANDP and MAOGA, Janis Ware, the executive director of the Summech Community Development Corporation, boosted the production of new and rehabbed affordable housing. The CODA streetscape and plaza upgrades along Ralph David Abernathy Boulevard helped to frame a revitalization strategy for the neighborhood. Over time, Summech has built hundreds of affordable residential units as the neighborhood continues to revitalize.

Recently, the Abernathy streetscape program has extended through the West End business district, gradually providing the kinds of upgrades necessary to address lower-wealth areas' needs for better infrastructure. And similar CODA efforts enhanced the civic gateways to the Atlanta University Center campuses farther to the west, which are described later.

In retrospect, CODA's work represented a remarkable spurt of achievement in a city not known for efficient delivery of capital projects and all on a $77 million budget and a three-year delivery ultimatum. The CODA streetscape and park improvements are in good order and continue to provide a model for major extensions of their high-quality designs, improving the public environment in an ever-expanding ring around their initial installation. Other neighborhoods in the ring took advantage of the growing Olympics momentum to undertake revitalization efforts.

CODA's staff for these achievements contributed mightily. Mostly just minted with master's degrees from Georgia Tech, these included Stan Harvey, Bob Begle, Danita Brown, John Threadgill, Tamara Williams, Doug Young and Ginny Kennedy. CODA staff not only provided the energy and talent to help get Atlanta through the Games but also continued to provide the continuity to carry many of the initiatives forward into the post-Olympic era. They have all gone on to productive and civic-minded careers, constituting yet another dimension of the legacy of the Games.

Summerhill

The Summerhill neighborhood housed some of the most intensive Olympic run-up activity. The neighborhood already had in place the Summerhill Neighborhood Development Corporation (SNDC), led by Doug Dean. Like the other neighborhoods in the ring, SNDC was a nonprofit organization. The corporation came into existence at the time when the Atlanta–Fulton County Recreation Authority built the home field stadium for the Atlanta Braves. It negotiated what can be called an impact-mitigation agreement in which funds generated by stadium parking provided a base of revenue for SNDC. Thus, with the proposal to create the Olympic Stadium over the three blocks farther south, the prospective effect on the neighborhood represented an extensive further incursion into the neighborhood and a challenge for maintaining stability and identity.

On the stadium site itself, as mentioned in chapter 3, neighborhood leaders Columbus Ward and Vincent Fort and AFL-CIO officer Stewart Acuff, after a series of actions, demonstrations and threats of camp-ins on the stadium site, were able to gain a modicum of success with an agreement with ACOG to hire 150 unemployed neighborhood people to work on the stadium.

Concurrent with the ACOG-managed stadium project, a significant private sector initiative by John Wieland Homes sought to establish a new development model, building sixty or so new houses on the lands just to the east of the stadium site's parking lots. Joining that development was that of the Greenlea Commons apartment complex by the state-chartered Metropolitan Atlanta Olympic Games Authority, headed by George Berry and staffed by Greg Pridgeon. These two projects represented the first significant new residential investments in the neighborhood in decades.

Vine City and English Avenue

Over in the Vine City and English Avenue neighborhoods, meanwhile, west of the Georgia World Congress Center, other ventures achieved some progress in housing development and neighborhood uplift. These neighborhoods had earlier been devastated by the destruction of their sister neighborhood to the east, Lightning, to make way for the land on which the GWCC had been built. Neighborhood-based CDCs formed and continued efforts to achieve grassroots improvements. These included the Vine City Housing Ministries led by Reverend W.L. Cotrell and Greg Hawthorn; the Bethursday Group, led by Reverend Cameron Alexander, Joe Beasley and Bob Jones; and Tyler Place, led by Carrie Salvary.

Empowerment Zone

From the background of the Empowerment Zone as described in chapter 2, the city used that initiative to fund the completion of plans for another twenty-five inner-ring neighborhoods over the next five years, laying the comprehensive framework for prioritizing its all-too-scant infrastructure and housing support resources to sustain some momentum on Mayor Jackson's vision for revitalization. The Empowerment Zone program, in addition, helped address some basic public health deficiencies in its neighborhoods, creating and carrying out the Zap Asthma program and funding an extensive Fire Department program to supply smoke alarms in all inhabited structures in the zone.

The program was widely criticized, as it happened, for inefficiencies, questionable real estate dealings and for not bringing enough support to some existing businesses. While some of the criticisms were justified, the program itself, as experienced through the years by other federal programs aimed at leveling the playing field, suffered from the magnitude of its charge. Trying to make a dent in the structural causes of poverty in an economy where profit is the bottom line is a tall order, with few examples of success. Beyond the hurdles to development, the Empowerment Zone's laudable effort to democratize decision-making by bringing a long-disenfranchised citizenry into the process, though worth a shot, made its job yet more challenging.

All of the Olympic Ring and Empowerment Zone neighborhoods, however, faced strong headwinds in their efforts, working off of a base of long-neglected urban infrastructure, unemployment, deep poverty, entrenched racism, inadequate funding and the associated derision visited on them by the city's power elites. Yet they did achieve some success in their homegrown and community-serving commitments, building better capacity and neighborhood-centered organizations.

THE OLYMPIC RING

The ACOG Venues

For starters, what happened to the city's ACOG venues? The Renaissance Group did not reflect on the longevity of the venues, streetscape, parks, public arts or neighborhood planning and development achievements. Evaluations of Olympic cities always include the criterion of lasting value of their sports facility investments. Atlanta scores at the top on this one, particularly for those venues in the core city, with greater sustained use, greater catalytic effect and lesser cost than most other Olympic cities.

One of the most enduring Olympic legacies is that now, after twenty-five years, most of the venue work lives on, either as built, or as modified, or as replaced on site, responding to increased demand and shifting markets. According to the pre-Olympic plan, the Georgia World Congress Center (GWCC) Authority, the group in charge of Atlanta's state-owned convention center, expanded Centennial Olympic Park, laying the base for the planning and construction of major new attractions framing the park.

The Olympic Stadium site today, showing GSU's football and baseball stadium conversions with parking lots turning into mixed-use developments. *Jeb Dobbins.*

The Olympic Stadium, modified into the Turner Field baseball stadium as planned from the outset, is now modified again as the Georgia State University football stadium, with the remainder of the old Atlanta–Fulton County stadium drum wall becoming the GSU baseball stadium. The overall redevelopment project is part of an ambitious Carter development partnership resulting in a major mixed-use transformation of the parking lots and access streets. The Atlanta Braves, having occupied the field for some twenty years, moved to Cobb County, fifteen miles to the northwest.

The Omni Coliseum was replaced on site with the Philips Arena, home of the Atlanta Hawks. The Georgia Dome, home of the Atlanta Falcons until 2018, was replaced by the Mercedes-Benz Stadium next door to its south, and the dome was razed. The Natatorium on the Georgia Tech campus, closed in and expanded into the campus recreation center, and the Georgia Tech basketball arena, used for boxing events for the Olympics, still there, have seen major upgrades. Most of the other venues and parks are still functioning, serving neighborhoods and athletic needs at the Atlanta University Center campuses and in the Summerhill neighborhood.

Bottom line, the infusion of upgrades and new construction of athletic facilities and the athletes' village, coupled with the global exposure of Atlanta's athletic commitment, lifted already-effective marketing for hosting athletic events of all kinds to a higher level. We provide more detail on how a few of these have evolved here.

Centennial Olympic Park

As described in chapter 3, the construction of what would become the primary icon and principal gathering space of the Games originated from an ACOG meeting with Central Atlanta Progress in 1993. The State of Georgia, through the Georgia World Congress Center, under the leadership of Dan Graveline, built, manages and owns the twenty-one-acre park, for which it continues to add demand-driven upgrades.

Ever since, it has been the go-to venue for large outdoor events in addition to serving daily residents, tourists and downtown workers with more intimate and smaller scale play and picnic areas. From the Olympic Rings fountain splash pool to major musical performances to Atlanta Hawks and Falcons games and other athletics events' spectators, the park is a major and lasting contribution to city life. Among the larger of the ACOG initiatives, Centennial Olympic Park became even more vibrant after completing its major expansion in 1998, catalyzing a ring of development around it.

Omni Coliseum

One of Atlanta's major existing venues that attracted the Olympics to Atlanta in the first place, the Omni Coliseum, was the home of the Atlanta Hawks NBA basketball franchise. Upgraded for the Games, the facility's owner, the Atlanta–Fulton County Recreation Authority (AFCRA), replaced the facility on site in 1998, which is an interesting story. Anticipating the closing of the Olympics, in May 1994, the president of the Atlanta Hawks basketball franchise, Stan Kasten, informed Mayor Bill Campbell of the team's intention to leave its home in Omni Coliseum and relocate to Gwinnett County to the northeast.

With Downtown still facing an uncertain future, Mayor Campbell reached out to Hawks owner Ted Turner and insisted that if the team wanted to rebuild, it should do so on the Omni site or nearby—and in no way leave the city. Turner got the message. After extensive investigation of alternatives on or adjacent to the site, the city and the Hawks settled on replacing Omni Coliseum on site, agreeing to play elsewhere for a couple of years, including at the Olympics-upgraded Georgia Tech basketball arena, McCamish Pavilion. As complicated as these logistical challenges were, how to pay for the demolition and new construction of a twenty-thousand-seat arena was even more complicated, as the mayor insisted that no city general obligation bonds could be part of the funding mix.

Both the city and the Hawks went about creating the financing structure. At the direction of the mayor, his chief of staff, attorney Steve Labovitz, proposed a bond-financing device that used a tax surcharge on car rentals in College Park south of the city, located to serve now Hartsfield-Jackson Atlanta International Airport. Imposition of such a tax depended on agreement with the College Park, Fulton County and state enabling legislation, all high hurdles. Yet all parties approved, with the first tranche of payback dedicated to retiring debt on the arena construction, the second to Clayton County and the third and fourth going more flexibly for improvements and operations in the areas immediately around the arena. In addition, the Hawks were able to gain investment support from the Philips electronics corporation, among other investors. Philips Arena, now renamed State Farm Arena, has served as the Hawks' home since its opening in 1999, a hockey team along the way, and it hosts more than 150 music, entertainment and other sports events each year. In 2019, AFCRA constructed a series of major updates and upgrades to the facility.

The Georgia Dome

The Georgia Dome, owned by the GWCC, was another existing venue that impressed the IOC. It had served its purpose as a major sports and event venue since opening in 1992 with the Atlanta Falcons as its flagship tenant. The building featured a light, airy and luminescent fabric roof structure, a fine space for an array of activities, including two Olympic basketball arenas. In 2013, the owner of the Falcons, Arthur Blank, co-founder of Home Depot, induced the city and the GWCC to build a new stadium immediately to the south, now styled the Mercedes-Benz Stadium. That project destroyed the dome and replaced it with events parking along with parking-compatible park uses when not needed for parking.

The Olympic Village

The Olympic Village at Georgia Tech at the north edge of Downtown housed some sixteen thousand athletes, some in refurbished dormitories (not occupied by students in the summer) and some in a new high-rise complex built immediately adjacent to the campus to the south, all outfitted with new state-of-the-art communications infrastructure. On completion of the Games, the new high-rise structures became dormitories for Georgia State University students, whose academic campus was located in nearby Downtown. The property changed hands and became Georgia Tech dorms in 2011 after a total rehabilitation and the addition of a popular dining hall. These transformations are a lasting legacy of the Olympics' visit to Atlanta. They signaled and underscored both universities' commitment to go all in as residential campuses, with the rising occupancy introducing a new and much welcomed vitality in both Midtown and Downtown.

ACOG developed many smaller sports venues that served to add to or upgrade athletic facilities for the Atlanta University Center (AUC), Georgia

The Olympic Village as repurposed for Georgia Tech's North Avenue housing complex with cafeteria, and other amenities, adjacent to Centennial Place. *Jeb Dobbins.*

Tech and Georgia State, all supported by CODA connective infrastructure. Most of the other nearby venues and CODA parks improved for the Olympics are still functioning, serving their neighborhoods with green space amenities that had been lacking before.

The Atlanta University Center Consortium, the largest grouping of historic Black colleges and universities in the nation, received considerable attention, providing venues for events and benefitting from CODA's streetscape and connectivity projects. ACOG renovated Herndon Stadium and built Forbes Arena on the Morehouse College campus, serving multiple uses of which basketball is the anchor and Panthers Stadium on the Clark Atlanta University campus. These campuses, along with Spelman College and Morris Brown College, provided training facilities for Olympic athletes. Except for Herndon Stadium, all of the Olympics venues continue as major athletic facilities. Regrettably, the Herndon Stadium has fallen into disrepair, as its host college, Morris Brown, fell on hard times and is struggling to restore its former stature. CODA converted James P. Brawley Street in the heart of the campus into a grand pedestrian promenade, the access and the foreground for the AUC campuses' Woodruff Library, a thriving landmark today.

AUC Promenade, converting part of James P. Brawley Drive from cars to grand walkway connecting all campuses to the centrally shared Woodruff Library. *Jeb Dobbins.*

One unfortunate casualty in the land assembly was the demolition of a house that had been occupied by W.E.B. Du Bois, some of whose papers and records were still on site. June Mundy, a longtime civil rights and equity activist, was able to retrieve much of the material before demolition. Another casualty was the demise of the historic nerve center of civil rights activism, Pascal's restaurant (which the H.J. Russell Corporation built anew near its other interests on Northside Drive).

Beyond the Olympics venues, the campuses, through AUC's consortium, established in 1929, sought to better coordinate their individual purposes and strengths, as well as to strengthen their linkages to the mostly low-wealth neighborhoods around them. The consortium launched the University Community Development Corporation in 1999 with the intent of aiding surrounding neighborhoods in rehabbing and upgrading housing in the immediate neighborhoods around the campuses. Underfunded, under-resourced and facing a difficult task, the UCDC nonetheless did the best it could with the tools available to it in its rehab work.

The campuses looked for a boost with the Atlanta Development Authority's Historic Westside Village initiative in 1997. The proposed mixed-use development proposal called for new housing, shops and offices on land that had been assembled across MLK Jr. Drive from the campuses. The project languished for a time, though, with limited interest from the powers that control most of the city's investment capital, but ultimately picked up steam as new housing complexes and a Walmart began to meet market needs.

THE CODA-PLANNED AND -DEVELOPED streetscapes, well begun, have generated follow-on projects to improve and extend their reach on the campuses and particularly along Martin Luther King Jr. Drive. This is not to say that civic resources or infrastructure in these historically underinvested neighborhoods were brought up to the level enjoyed by more affluent neighborhoods to the north and east, only that the Olympic investments by ACOG and parallel investments through CODA and the city made a good start.

Beyond ACOG's venues and CODA's connective infrastructure, the intertwining partnerships that emerged from delivering on the Olympics mandate continued to deliver projects and programs in the Olympic Ring.

CENTRAL ATLANTA PROGRESS

Central Atlanta Progress was the lead player in forming most of the partnerships that fueled measured progress in reenergizing Downtown. CAP is the nonprofit business association representing the downtown portion of the core city. CAP's planning efforts from its beginnings were extensive, undertaking Central Area Studies and Olympic-era updates that continue on under the successive leadership of Sam Williams (during the Olympics), Charlie Battle, Rick Reinhart and A.J. Robinson. Anticipating the possibility for a catalytic effect generated through the Olympics opportunities, CAP undertook a series of planning and development initiatives, beginning with the work of Paul Kelman and followed by Jennifer Ball.

To help fund the ongoing implementation of its multiple planning and operational efforts, CAP succeeded in gaining business and property-owner support to establish its Community Improvement District, one of the first to take advantage of new state enabling legislation. Better-coordinated security, streetscape improvements, ongoing maintenance, parks and other development project support suited both CAP's and the city's goals. With the Olympics coming, yet with predictable business opposition to increasing taxes—albeit for a good cause and including a commitment to enhance public safety—would the initiative have passed if the Olympics were not an onrushing force? Maybe, maybe not, but clearly the Olympics would factor into business owners' vote. CAP persuaded businesses and property owners to meet the necessary approval thresholds to levy the property tax increment deemed necessary to address these goals. The oversight structure for the use and management of these funds included business leaders and a member of the city council. Subsequently, Midtown and Buckhead formed CIDs as major tools to co-guide their future development priorities with the city.

Moving on to the Tax Allocation District as another partnership tool, the city needed to replace a district that it had established through its Downtown Development Authority (now part of Invest Atlanta) before the Olympics. The one on the books was in an area of west Downtown dominated by parking lots punctuated by occasional deteriorating structures. When a brain wave reimagined most of that site as the future Centennial Olympic Park, most of the site came off of the tax rolls, and its viability as an economic development tool evaporated.

In the redrawing of the boundaries to make a TAD feasible, the city recognized the value of incentivizing new development in a broader area of Downtown. At the same time, though, the city wanted to share the bounty of development-driven tax revenue with the low-wealth neighborhoods west of Downtown that had been persistently ignored by big-ticket projects. Accordingly, the city required that a portion of the increment value be shared to support infrastructure improvements in those neighborhoods. Thus, the TAD was drawn to extend a mile to the west to encompass the Vine City and English Avenue neighborhoods, where 20 percent of the increment would be committed.

Negotiations went forward to shape that structure. The parties at the table included:

- the City of Atlanta planning department and its development authority
- CAP through the leadership of Ken Bleakly, its Centennial Olympic Park Area (COPA) director
- the neighborhoods led by Reverend Cameron Alexander and Joe Beasley from Antioch Missionary Baptist Church, Vine City Health and Housing Ministry director Greg Hawthorne under the leadership of Reverend W.L. Cotrell of Beulah Baptist Church, along with others

The negotiations were not necessarily easy, yet they yielded the desired result. The TAD was set up so that 20 percent of whatever increment was generated would be directed to meeting infrastructure needs and supporting neighborhood-serving development. The city council adopted the TAD ordinance. This TAD, then, approved in 1997, marked an early foray into seeking incremental and feasible ways to physically improve impoverished neighborhoods and diminish the wealth divide.

Framing Centennial Olympic Park

Another CAP initiative called for accelerating high-density development on the vacant properties that adjoined Centennial Olympic Park to the north, east and west. At the end of the Games, with the north half of the park still unfinished, the area around was bleak—parking lots, vacant lots and no edge to frame the park properly as it sloped down gradually beyond its designated boundary on Baker Street. Jim Vaseff, an architect/urbanist working for Georgia Power and a participant in the review process, noted the lack of suitable framing for the park by comparing it with Boston Commons, whose clear and distinctive delineation of public and private added to its attraction.

As the north half of the park was nearing completion, Coca-Cola, working with the city, purchased the land farther to the north, across Baker Street, with the idea of creating new cultural and entertainment attractions that could frame the park. For the purchase to encompass the land necessary to accommodate future entertainment venues, though, the city needed to abandon two existing two-lane streets, Simpson and Jones. Working with attorney Larry Dingle on behalf of Coke, the city was able to avoid the kind of tussles that often occur in these kinds of street right-of-way claims and forge an agreement that served the interests of both. The two parties agreed to swap out the land released by abandoning the two streets for a comparable swath of land to widen the north boundary street, now Ivan Allen Drive, to provide a clearer and more serviceable four-lane bridge connecting the west side neighborhoods with downtown. Further, at a time when the region was barred from using federal transportation funds for capacity-improving projects because of air quality standards noncompliance, the city was able to make the case that because of the swap-out, capacity was not being increased. Accordingly, GDOT was able to put the new arterial on the state route, which allowed the use of federal funds in its construction.

Thus, to Vaseff's point, the city and CAP worked on two fronts to frame the park and position it as a prime asset for pumping new life and investment into the area. They used the recently created Special Public Interest (SPI) zoning district to encourage active, mixed-use and institutional redevelopment in a way that indeed would properly frame the park and its vistas. To assist in financing the desired results, they were able to use the TAD described earlier. The facilities then erected on the north side of Baker Street provided the desired frame. Coca-Cola planned and developed a World of Coke venue to replace an existing smaller such space across from the state capitol. They negotiated with the city, CAP and major project funder Bernie Marcus, co-founder of Home Depot, to build the Georgia Aquarium. Funded largely by Marcus with TAD support from the city, the Georgia Aquarium joined the World of Coke, which itself received significant TAD funding, as the north frame for the park. Both are constant attractions to large numbers of tourists and locals alike. The

Ivan Allen Jr. Bridge connecting west side neighborhoods into Downtown, with newly dedicated artwork and the Georgia Aquarium in the background. *Jeb Dobbins*.

Frisbee in front of the Center for Civil and Human Rights, one of the venues framing the north edge of Centennial Olympic Park. *Jeb Dobbins*.

Centennial Olympic Park now, looking north, the centerpiece of growing intensity in Downtown Atlanta. *Gene Phillips Photography.*

balance of the Coca-Cola land has since served for the expansion of the aquarium and as the site for the Center for Civil and Human Rights.

The center highlights the historic and ongoing struggles for social equity, in which Atlanta has a strong, pivotal, but not yet fully attained history. A core treasure in the center is the archive of native son Martin Luther King Jr., which, along with other material, makes it a prominent resource for study and research on the civil rights and other social justice movements.

GEORGIA STATE UNIVERSITY

GSU president Carl Patton viewed Downtown with its Olympic boost as a rich opportunity to transform the campus. From its inception, GSU had been a commuter campus with scant living facilities and an intentional walling off of its campus from the "big, bad, and scary downtown" outside of its walls. Patton, beginning at the time of the Olympics run-up, utterly reversed that culture, in attitude, development strategy and impact. Patton, who holds a master's degree in city and regional planning and a doctorate in public policy from UC Berkeley, undertook a comprehensive master plan to guide the university's conversion to a full-blown residential research university, fully integrated and interconnected with its surroundings, a campus of the streets.

Patton then turned the core campus inside out with investments in Downtown that stabilized what at the time was still a lag in investment attraction. He was an active member of CAP, serving as its chairman for

Muse's Loft, viewed from Woodruff Park, an early foray in upper story residential conversions, Olympics-era home of Gretchen and Carl Patton, president of GSU. *Jeb Dobbins*.

several years. He and his wife's bold move to sell GSU's presidents' mansion in Buckhead and buy into Muse's Loft, the city's and CAP's untested loft conversion strategy, dramatically underscored his commitment to and engagement with this special urban neighborhood.

GSU's presence and continuing expansion has played a major part in Downtown's transformation. And again, the question: without the city's, CAP's and CODA's visible actions to prepare the city for the Games, would such bold moves by Georgia State have been likely, or even politically or financially possible?

Centennial Olympic Park Area (COPA)

In 1995, looking to spread the opportunity of the moment, CAP created the Centennial Olympic Park Area Inc., under the leadership of Ken Bleakly, with the intent of initiating development activity to its edges of influence. As noted earlier, Bleakly was CAP's point person in establishing the downtown TAD. Prime among these opportunities was the Northyards, formerly a CSX predecessor rail companies' maintenance facility and freight yards complex. With its unique form generated by its historic roundhouse, the site had only marginal use at the time of the Olympics.

The vision here, formed out of an American Institute of Architects' Regional/Urban Development Assistance Team (R/UDAT), was to create a research-and-development incubator campus on largely obsolescent and underutilized lands in the northwest corner of downtown, across the CSX freight rail artery from Coca-Cola's corporate headquarters and across North Avenue from the southwestern flank of the Georgia Tech campus. Emerging market trends seemed to hold out hope that demand could begin to fill out the northwest corner of Downtown. It took some time for the pace of development to pick up. Along the way, Georgia Tech partnered with Northyards through the University Finance Foundation to add to its extensive laboratory and research centers with a multistory lab facility. Now, though, the site has become a key connective hub for new affordable housing, Georgia Tech continued research expansion, and the growing opportunity to use its assets to bridge the race and class divide across Northside Drive. These collaborations are committed to finding ways to bend their resources and amenities to provide a welcoming gateway to the neighborhoods to the west.

OTHER CORE CITY PARTNERSHIP INITIATIVES

Meanwhile, new development and renewed development continue to occur in the core. The city eliminated the down ramps that had blocked safe pedestrian crossing between the Philips Arena and the convention center by lifting the street. The city, Turner Properties, the GWCC and the Metro Chamber, a fronting property, rebuilt Andrew Young International Boulevard in order to create a "complete street," slowing traffic and prioritizing pedestrian accessibility. The result is greatly improved pedestrian connections between the park, the GWCC, the arena and the new attractions that keep popping up. The existing Omni Hotel doubled its size with a major addition. The latest addition was the opening in 2014 of the College Football Hall of Fame south of the park, which is filling the attraction gap between the GWCC, Philips Arena, the park itself and the other developments and attractions that now ring the park. Altogether, millions of people visit these points of interest every year.

Soon after the Olympics, Legacy Properties—led by David Marvin and supported significantly by a city real estate tax abatement—began to build out its block adjacent to the northwest of the Centennial Olympic Park, with a major hotel, restaurants and retail space, followed by condominium development. And to the northeast, the twenty-two-story Museum Tower condo project rose, anchored at its base by a children's museum. These efforts together filled in what had been mainly parking and vacant lots. These developments used the SPI zoning district as the regulatory tool and tax abatements and the TAD as funding resources.

The Multimodal Passenger Terminal (MMPT)

Anticipating the Olympics, efforts were underway in the early '90s to create a "Multimodal Passenger Terminal" (MMPT), slated for "The Gulch," in which the planning called for a transportation hub linking commuter rail, intercity bus, MARTA rail, local bus, automobiles and possible intercity rail. The Gulch is the name given to the vast array of Norfolk Southern and CSX freight rail lines that intersect at the ground level, separating Downtown from Castleberry Hill and other neighborhoods to the south and west. The street level is about forty feet above the track level, providing the space needed to accommodate all of the different transit modes. The street level, then, would provide for intensive mixed-use, mixed-income development, taking advantage of unsurpassed transportation access. The desired outcome would be to create the center for a commuter rail network with direct linkages between local transit and intercity travel. Downtown would find an intensive, vibrant and focusing development that would cover over the gash of the Gulch, creating seamless connectivity to the nearby neighborhoods.

Hal Wilson at GDOT, Dobbins at the city and Catherine Ross at the Georgia Regional Transportation Authority (GRTA), with consultant support, determined that the project was sufficiently feasible to proceed to the next phase, albeit with daunting technical, organizational, political and financial obstacles. Because of the complexity of its challenges, the project was slated to start with the modest first phase of providing a small commuter rail station in the nearer term, with rudimentary but functional connectivity, while continuing with planning for other phases. The project included the first phase of a commuter line to the south, ending in Lovejoy and aimed toward Griffin as a next phase stop. Congressman John Lewis had secured some $89 million of federal funds to jumpstart the project. A resolution to enter into an agreement with GDOT to pursue next steps was on the city council consent agenda for adoption in its first meeting of the 2002 session.

Cathy Woolard, then city council president, however, took the resolution off the consent agenda, and it was never considered again. By then, she had become an all-in advocate for the latest version of the emerging BeltLine project and apparently felt that the MMPT project would somehow detract from or compete with it, even though the transportation purpose and funding streams were not in conflict.

Other serious efforts have been mounted to sustain or advance the MMPT concept. Central Atlanta Progress's "Greenline" project saw a powerful vision for knitting the GWCC and the Georgia Dome with the state capitol, knitting the north and south sides of the CBD across the freight rail tracks, thus providing seamless connectivity between downtown, GSU and the government centers along with a shared linear park space. In 2015, GDOT mounted a thoroughgoing development proposal, again along a green space frame that, like the earlier proposals, not only covered the gulch and the freight rail tracks but also would have directly connected the west side neighborhood with the core of Downtown. With lots of community input along the way, GDOT posted its proposals on its website. Within a few hours, though, the proposal was taken down, reportedly at the behest of Governor Deal, with no reason given.

The Gulch, the railroad interchange and historic divide between Downtown and nearby neighborhoods, the opportunity for transportation and civic connectivity. *Jeb Dobbins.*

Most recently, a Los Angeles–based developer, the CIM group, has succeeded in entering into contract with the city to take control of the whole Gulch property with the intent of building a major mixed-use project over many years, starting with a modest first phase. The city council voted to provide over $1 billion of subsidy to the project. Over the years, the city has experienced robust growth with the twin downsides of a rising number of its citizens living in poverty or priced out by gentrification. The city council, however, voted to provide the exorbitant subsidy to the project, despite its token support for housing, jobs and health needs, and to abandon the MMPT transportation hub concept forever.

In the larger picture, both in Atlanta and nationally, the employment of such public resource-enhancing devices reflects the national lurch toward privatization, often in the form of private-public partnerships. The cachet of privatization was "to run government like a business," whose progenitors' underlying purpose, in fact, was to divert more tax dollars from public accountability to private control and thus gain. This trend theoretically could produce results that serve both a public and a private purpose. But for many years the diversion of funds from public to private hands has been eroding the city's capability to adequately build and maintain its public realm, to prioritize its resources to where community need is greatest, and to monitor and strengthen all the public-serving provisions in its regulatory and funding agreements.

Olympic Ring Housing

Very little residential development occurred Downtown after World War II through the early 1990s, as Downtown experienced the outmigration of jobs and residents typical of other cities in that period. With the presence of most of the Olympic venues in Downtown, however, this dynamic changed dramatically. Almost five hundred units were developed in the pre-Olympic period. Immediately following the Games, the new trend continued with brand-new residential development and conversions of underutilized commercial space into residential lofts. What mainly drove this sudden surge in residential repurposing was in fact the Olympics, with their promise of generating a high-end market with hopes for over-the-top revenue, albeit for a four-week period.

Loft Conversions

More generally, interacting with the Olympics run-up and aftermath, the city and lenders upped their support for the conversion of many other older loft-type structures, mostly vacant or underutilized by their former light industrial and warehousing functions.

The Fairlie-Poplar "neighborhood" in the center of Downtown, for example, abutting Woodruff Park to its east and Centennial Olympic Park to its west, found growing advocacy for transforming its special grid of streets into a renewed mixed-use and more diverse and vibrant district. Before the Olympics, with its narrow streets, two-hundred-foot-square blocks, a number of charming but underutilized buildings and lots of parking lots and garages, it appeared to provide just the kind of framework attractive to the emerging centrification markets. But the area had not yet managed to garner the forward winds of a "new urban" trending market with its old urban market offerings.

With the vision and sustained leadership of Stuart Peebles, the Fairlie-Poplar Task Force, under the wing of CAP, was able to support and drive a transformation process in the Olympic run-up that continues today. As mentioned, the loft buildings fronting on Peachtree with long-neglected upper floors transformed into residences, opening just before the Olympics. Jim Cummings purchased the "flatiron" building, shaped by the skewed intersection of Peachtree, and Broad and converted it into "edgy" office spaces. The Healey building, a pre–World War I sixteen-story "skyscraper" in the Gothicesque style, and the William-Oliver building, a 1930s skyscraper in the art deco style, among others, went through similar conversion, repurposing their former office functions into condos or apartments. Georgia State University began to sprinkle some of its departments and classrooms into the district, further building on the incremental path toward mixed-use repopulation and an energetic bustle.

Fairlie-Poplar also was the first area to benefit from the new TAD district, with the support of the new, pleasingly contextual midrise condo at 123 Luckie Street. This project was right across Spring Street (now Ted Turner Drive) from Ted's Montana Grill on the ground floor and the Turner Foundation offices above, with Ted Turner's penthouse at the top. Across Luckie Street, environmentalist Turner covered a surface parking lot with an extensive array of solar collectors.

123 Luckie Street, the first new built condominium in Fairlie-Poplar, supported by TAD funding. Ted Turner's Ted's Montana Grill is in the background, home of his foundation and surmounted by his penthouse. *Jeb Dobbins.*

Castleberry Hill

Other loft conversion activity began to occur in the Castleberry Hill neighborhood, south and across the Gulch from Downtown. Back in the old days, the neighborhood was known as "Snake Nation," a colorful moniker for sometimes violent confrontations of its rough and tumble "Rowdy Party" with the more genteel "Moral Party."[*] Its subsequent loft building growth resulted in a fairly cohesive building inventory that became attractive to artists, precursors of "maker spaces," and for homeless shelters.

Atlanta has traditions of developers moving into unlikely places to test out the possibility of emerging markets. In this case, Bruce Gallman and Larry Miller began buying up some of the loft buildings and converting them into apartments, many later converted to condominiums. They were able to persuade lenders of their belief in the viability of the markets, notably Jim Mynott at SunTrust Bank, to try a kind of nontraditional and seemingly risky financing package. At the same time, the whole loft conversion process depended on being able to garner city regulatory support. The city had at the time, and actually through the whole span of the Olympic era, a chief building official named Norman Koplon, who was far more committed to experimentation than his counterparts in that position in most cities. Koplon's driving principle was to figure out how to make things work in the spirit and purpose of the multiple codes involved in building permitting, not how to say "no," the more usual building official response in many cities.

In the case of the Castleberry Hill neighborhood, Gary Foy was the champion. Another activist and early investor in the district, Jim Schneider, had a deep understanding of the regulatory processes binding the city and was able to use this knowledge in supportive ways. The neighborhood followed up the city's post-Olympics program commitment to neighborhood plans through its Empowerment Zone funding. The city engaged architect David Butler, who crafted a sensible and useful plan and project process that has helped shape the neighborhood's incremental preservation and repurposing of existing buildings as well as redeveloping other sites in the spirit of its historic character.

A key test for neighborhood muscle and city planning support came in the wake of the onset of loft conversions. In 2002, the National Association of Homebuilders held its conference in Atlanta. The themes included repurposing older buildings for residential use, seeking to

---

[*] *Atlanta Magazine*, 2014.

orient members toward the potentials of this new market or to build models that were compatible with loft and other types of contextual environments. To prepare examples for the conference, the association commissioned Andres Duany, of new urbanism fame, to design what such a compatible model might look like, which it would then build. He came up with three side-by-side live-work-type units on Peters Street in Castleberry Hill. They worked pretty well in context but for one glaring variation: he insisted that the roofs had to be pitched, consistent with his new urbanist form kit of parts. The neighborhood, already listed as historic, led by Foy, counter-insisted that the roofs had to be flat, like all the other roofs in the neighborhood. The city planning department called for a meeting to resolve what had become an impasse for moving forward to approval. The department, notwithstanding Duany's stature, approved the neighborhood's position, and Duany opted to get his slope aspirations represented by sloping "eyebrows" affixed below the parapets of the now flat-roofed buildings.

The district has become a major center for the arts, with galleries, studios and events giving special flavor to the now mixed-use and vital neighborhood. Tragically, as the neighborhood was regenerating itself, Foy was gunned down at a convenience store at the edge of the neighborhood.

Castleberry Hill, National Association of Home Builders–sponsored venture into infill housing: live-work units designed by Andres Duany, 2002. *Jeb Dobbins.*

Notable for Atlanta in both Castleberry Hill and in Fairlie-Poplar are two characteristics. Both framed their futures based on a vision, a planful approach and a locally invested champion to move the revitalization forward. And both, however consciously, oversaw incremental processes with the effect of attenuating speculation and tax increases that in other parts of the city have become more disruptive.

Cotton Mill Lofts

Meanwhile, immediately across the tracks and south of Old Fourth Ward at the edge of the Cabbagetown neighborhood, another creative community-spirited developer, John Aderhold, set forth to convert the historic closed-down Fulton Cotton Mill into residential loft apartments. Enormously complicated projects, these loft conversion properties have to overcome barriers in financing, constructing and marketing, as well as creativity in their zoning and building permit approvals. Like in Fairlie-Poplar and Castleberry Hill, chief building official Norman Koplon approached these kinds of ventures with the attitude of "what's it gonna take to get it done," rather than "doesn't meet code, forget about it," occasionally the attitude of building officials elsewhere.

CITIZENS' INITIATIVES

Certainly linked in various ways to the new consciousness of what the city could be post-Olympics, other transformational initiatives, many of them based on citizen activism, arose out of the increasing visibility and appreciation of the CODA work and the city's commitment and capability to support the follow-up. A distinguishing feature of Atlanta's culture is the will of individuals to seize one or another issue not adequately addressed in city policy, priority and action. However coincidental, the Olympics moment stirred up or accelerated attention toward some of these issues, whose champions showed remarkable persistence and passion to see their initiatives addressed and largely incorporated into receiving mainstream city program support.

Pedestrians: Pedestrians Educating Drivers on Safety (PEDS)

Care for the quality and safety of the pedestrian environment became a central concern among citizens, particularly those most afflicted by the abysmal quality of the city's sidewalks and pedestrian neglect more generally. Pedestrian injuries and fatalities seemed to be on the rise when a woman named Sally Flocks stepped into the breach. She mounted an impassioned one-woman campaign that led to more and more support, forming an organization called PEDS, Pedestrians Educating Drivers on Safety, in 1996. Her work was touted by the city planning department but slow to gain traction in the public works department, which had the whip hand in actually carrying out the sensible things she was proposing. But little by little, with major boosting from growing numbers of citizens and then city council members, the department ramped up a more pedestrian-friendly program. She proceeded to hook into like-minded local organizations around the country, her growing expertise respected and sought after nationally.

Bikes

Two strong centers of advocacy for promoting bicycles emerged during the Olympic moment. The PATH Foundation, led by Ed McBrayer and founded in 1991, not only advocated but actually produced miles of off-street bicycle trails, using park areas and abandoned rail corridors. McBrayer's aim was to provide a safe, family-friendly amenity that served both the casual rider and also commuter traffic. Funded mainly by philanthropy, his work continues, and its success has significantly boosted what was already a rising tide of bicycles.

Also in 1991, the Atlanta Bicycle Campaign, led by Dennis Hoffarth and Barbara McCann, dedicated its resources particularly to making existing streets safer for bike use. The target was more the commuter cyclist than the family. It achieved a succession of changes in bikes' rights to the road, like making storm drain grates perpendicular rather than parallel with the travel path and a whole range of street markings and signage that have greatly improved bikeability in the city. His legacy carries forward under the leadership of Rebecca Serna, who has further boosted bikes' future in the city with a succession of "Streets Alive" events, continuing and improving bike lane infrastructure throughout.

Trees: Trees Atlanta

In anticipation of the Games' arrival, the city and CAP launched a tree-planting program aimed at planting ten thousand trees. Even though Atlanta is a city in a woodland, its core areas were barren, imparting a particularly bleak and uninviting terrain for the millions of visitors expected for the Games. Among other tree planting initiatives, the city passed an ordinance that required parking lot owners in the downtown area to install in their lots one tree for every eight parking spaces. Of course, a great howl arose from the affected property owners and parking operator lessees. Crying foul, they sought to obstruct the applicability of the ordinance in general and in particular because of its retroactive application. With city attorney Robert Zoeckler and others in the Law Department carrying the case for the city, lower courts found for the city, based on the ordinance's provision for couching the city's action in a clear policy framework. The case was appealed all the way to the Supreme Court, whose inaction allowed the lower courts' findings to stand. Thus, the city prevailed, trees got planted, and the city softened and shaded its downtown.

Identifying tree planting as an important city and downtown priority, CAP joined with and supported attorney Marcia Bansley, who founded Trees Atlanta in 1985, choosing to redirect her mission from the law to her passion. She was resolute, productive and effective in her pursuit, wherever and whatever it took. The organization she formed gained more and more philanthropic support, an enabling attitude in city hall and thus more and more trees, a visible triumph and a dent in Atlanta's heat island.

The realization of the importance of tree protection and tree installation for preserving the city's character as a city in a threatened woodland combined with mitigating the "heat island" effect grew ever greater numbers of citizen supporters. Their advocacy, spearheaded by architect Sheldon Schlegman, led in 2000 to the city's adoption of its first tree ordinance along with funding for two urban forester positions in the building department. One of the early hires for a spot was a man named Tom Coffin, who earlier as a counterculture activist had been an editor of *The Great Speckled Bird*, a revered rag for the maturing Atlanta hippy and counterculture community. His work as the tree enforcer was vigorous and effective, while sometimes over the top.

The Chattahoochee River

On another Olympics-era action front, citizen activism over the degradation of water quality on the river led to the founding of the Upper Chattahoochee Riverkeeper in 1994 by Rutherford and Laura Turner Seidel under the leadership of Sally Bethea. Through environmental litigation and state legislation, the city landed in a consent decree requiring it to begin to fix the problem. The city's storm and sanitary systems had been neglected for decades, worsening in the out-of-sight, out-of-mind jinx that underground systems so often experience. The city embarked on a comprehensive billion-dollar upgrade to its R.M. Clayton sewer treatment plant and began the process of upgrading its sewer system network with an infill and infiltration program. This work brought downstream Chattahoochee River water quality up to an acceptable level after decades of neglect, and the too-skinny fish in West Point Lake downriver began to put on weight.

At the same time, the city, with the leadership of city planning staff member Alycen Whiddon, reinforced its commitment to the river and its estuarine environment by partnering with the Trust for Public Land to secure either fee title or protective easements on river-fronting properties in the city downstream from the Clayton plant. Later on, these beginnings led to protecting tributaries to "The Chatt" and a special bond election in Shirley Franklin's mayoralty that provided $4 billion for a comprehensive overhaul of the water supply and storm and sanitary systems. The opportunities to advance public use of Atlanta's defining watersheds and creeks as walking trails, however, languished over concerns that too much traffic and enjoyment of these as natural recreational assets might harm aquatic life and downstream water quality.

MIDTOWN

The Olympic Ripple Spreads North

Catching the Olympic wind, Midtown Alliance, the business interests representing the northern portion of the city's core, initiated a major planning effort called Blueprints Midtown. This area of the core contained a few signature developments, like the Woodruff Arts Center, Colony Square,

BellSouth's corporate headquarters and other commercial one-offs, but all were disconnected, pockmarked with random parking lots and scattered commercial activity. Georgia Tech was across the divide of the "Downtown Connector," a world apart. The Alliance hired urban designer Anton Nelessen to manage the process, and he was able to use new technology, "visual preference surveys" with computer feedback, to guide the Alliance toward priorities and ultimately consensus to move the plan forward.

The city made clear that for its full support the Alliance should conduct an inclusive and transparent process, including full neighborhood and small enterprise participation. With backing from executive director Susan Mendheim, board member Steve Nygren and others, the ensuing progress gained strong support from the city, which facilitated incorporating the plans into the city's Comprehensive Development Plan. The policy in place, then, laid the base for the city to rezone the whole of the area into Special Public Interest (SPI) districts with a range of context-based subarea parts. This planning effort launched a successful ongoing redevelopment process that transformed the area, in which Shannon Powell as urban design and developer director for the Alliance played the implementation role.

CODA, the city and CAP transformed Peachtree Street Downtown into a quality boulevard just in time for the Games. The Alliance moved to extend that tree-lined, elegantly lit system all the way north through Midtown. This extension completed the transformation of the Downtown-Midtown linear city core as the city's iconic signature thoroughfare. The Blueprints plan further reinforced the formalistic grid of the other north–south and east–west streets, recognizing their hierarchy according to density, connectivity beyond and the need for distinguished streetscape design to further spur reinvestment. The character and the purpose of this work initiated similarly thoughtful and distinctive lane removals, replaced with streetscape treatments on other Midtown streets with priority for the north–south streets. Thus Piedmont Avenue was improved, significantly funded through a Livable Centers Initiative grant from the Atlanta Regional Commission (about which more later) and in conjunction with better defining and dressing up its Piedmont Park frontage.

The City Planning Department and Midtown Alliance collaborated to wrest control over the public's right-of-way from just the car to a better balance for humanizing the pedestrian and landscape environment. The goal was to reduce the number of travel lanes from six to four on major north–south arterial streets. The idea was to use the liberated street space to install bulb-outs at the corners to reduce pedestrian crossing distances and to provide on-street parking in between. The first test of this idea came with the Midtown Lofts project, a mixed-use midrise apartment development facing West Peachtree in a Tech Square revitalization that was just beginning to happen. The planning department made this new treatment a condition for the project's approval. The developer understood the merit and the value of that requirement and built it that way. But the City Public Works Department had a fit. The department had signed off on the lane removal and streetscape treatment plans, but they may not have understood the plans as drawn. When public works staff saw the result on the ground, they sought to force the developer to tear it up and return the street to its prior six lane cross-section. Ultimately, the mayor affirmed the work as installed, thus setting the precedent for other lane removal and streetscape treatments on this and other north–south avenues through Midtown.

The key roles of the City in its partnership with Midtown Alliance depended on its adoption of a broadly inclusive approach to shape policies and practices. The Alliance, like CAP, instituted its own Community Improvement District, which along with the Comprehensive Development Plan and the SPI zoning in place, stimulated and supported development activity. This framework, along with major variously funded streetscape and other infrastructure upgrades, began knitting together forlorn vacant lots and adding to the area's assets.

Early venture into replacing travel lanes with parallel parking, landscaping and shorter pedestrian crossings at Midtown Lofts in Tech Square. *Jeb Dobbins.*

As a legacy of the city's insistence on inclusion, development projects as they unfolded were subject to a development review committee whose advisory opinion guided the city's granting of Special Administrative Permits as a condition for attaining building permits. The make-up of this committee included four members named by the larger, more diverse, residentially based Neighborhood Planning Unit and three named by the Alliance, thus ensuring that proposed projects responded to community guidance, not just private-sector, project-only interests. What began as a belief and sense of the place as a mostly commercial and corporate investment attraction rather swiftly transformed into a mainly high-density, middle- and upper-middle-range residential development bonanza.

The span of this work, east–west from Piedmont Park to Georgia Tech and north–south from Buckhead to Downtown, reinforced the linear definition of the city and the potential for greater connectivity among the three areas. Picking up on this larger vision for the Peachtree spine, Scotty Greene, executive director of the then recently formed Buckhead Community Improvement District, launched with city support regular but informal meetings with his counterparts in Midtown and CAP. The purpose, not unlike the city's coordination meetings with diverse agencies described earlier, was to share information on activities, look for areas of synergies or of competitive overlap and build on the strengths that each of the three districts offered.

Unexpected in 1997 when the Blueprints-inspired redevelopment process took off, the urban-living surge led Midtown Alliance to launch Blueprints II in 2002, a mid-course correction in priority to take advantage of the high-density, mixed-use, amenity-rich "neighborhood" that the area was becoming. This plan emphasized lining the widened sidewalk frontages of Peachtree with retail, termed the "miracle mile." Improved street fronting retail on other north–south streets became a priority as well. The significant rise in property values and the "newness" of retail in this location, however, slowed developers' and owners' ability to properly subsidize rents to achieve a true popular mix of retail spaces, obstacles that the Alliance committed itself to overcome.

Georgia Tech

It was in this same time frame that Georgia Tech and Midtown greatly strengthened their physical, economic and cultural connections.

Paralleling GSU's radical transformation, Wayne Clough, a GT alum and also a UC Berkeley grad, became the president of GT in 1994. He inherited a physical and cultural campus that shared many of GSU's pre-Olympics characteristics. The campus, while residential with dormitories and Greek houses, had eschewed any direct physical connectivity with its surroundings, presenting instead a them-and-us defensive posture. In the Olympic run-up, Clough began to steer the campus culture away from protected bastion to community-wide resource. Building on its role as the Olympic Village and beneficiary of major venue construction, the campus began to interconnect itself with the city, beginning in Midtown.

In 1996, the campus commissioned the WRT consultancy to develop a master plan to guide its efforts for major upgrades and better cohesiveness in meeting its own growing enrollment and program complexity. The plan proposed policy and physical planning shifts, anticipating connectivity to Midtown across I-75/85 to the east and across North Avenue to the south, essentially reaching out a hand to its flanking neighborhoods. Dobbins, representing the city, participated in the master planning process at the invitation of the College of Architecture's dean, Tom Galloway.

As part of this expansive planning vision was Tech's serious consideration of building its way across the Downtown Connector into Midtown. One of the trustees of the Georgia Tech Foundation, Charles Brown (who was also the initiator of the Atlantic Station project, about which more later), had been pushing for the campus to make this move for some time. He proposed, among other initiatives, buying the old and unused historic Biltmore Hotel for Tech's administrative center and in general buying up properties as they might come available. The Biltmore idea didn't fly, but the Novare Group, led by Jim Borders, bought the property and refurbished and retrofitted it for offices with a rooftop penthouse to reinforce this connection to Midtown.

The "Downtown Connector," I-75/85, a depressed three-hundred-foot-wide roadway carrying some 400,000 cars per day, divided the campus from Midtown, a gash in the city fabric. The terrain on the Midtown side of the gash was derelict—parking lots, vacant lots, a scattering of down-at-the-heels, under-occupied buildings, broken fences, weeds, syringes, condoms, blowing paper.

The linchpin that consolidated the interrelationships between Georgia Tech and Midtown was the rebuilding of the Fifth Street Bridge across the Downtown Connector. The bridge itself was a two-lane street with parking and five-foot-wide sidewalks and chain-link fences on either side. Altogether a dismal, loud, and even scary prospect for the few students who ventured across.

As the Tech Square initiative made its way from vision to projects, one of the partners in the venture, developer Kim King, began pushing the idea of a major overhaul to the bridge. Georgia Tech's Midtown projects were underway at this point, mostly on the south side of Fifth Street from the Connector to West Peachtree Street. King, a Cobb County suburban commercial developer, had reset his development aspirations toward denser, more connected models that were emerging as attractive for urban markets. He was putting together a deal on the north side of Fifth for a private/ Tech partnership to provide commercial space, business incubator space and others of Tech's economic generator initiatives.

King was a Tech grad, a storied one at that as the star quarterback of a couple of Tech's more successful football teams. Beyond that, he had been the chairman of the finance committee for Governor Roy Barnes's election campaign. With induced buy-in from the state in the form of GDOT, Georgia Tech, Midtown and the city moved rather quickly to turn the idea into a project. King's first thought was that the bridge's ideal look would be arches spanning the freeway, painted Georgia Tech yellow. Hesitation rose from the other participants, however, none comfortable with evoking the fast food chain.

The design process set forth in earnest, and through a series of iterations, the different organizational participants came up with a concept that met the complex technical requirements. First, the new bridge needed to become a park, tree-lined, green, well-lighted, space for outdoor events and lounging, in short replacing the grim with an attractive connective gateway. GDOT took the opportunity to widen and lift the bridge to accommodate a possible widening of the Connector below. Figuring out how to design a structure to achieve those goals was daunting. The project had to accommodate park spaces on either side of the widened sidewalks with shade-giving trees, other plantings and suitable lighting, as well as block the deafening roar of the traffic that daily passed underneath. And it had to do all that while maintaining traffic access during construction and not unduly interfere with traffic flows on the Connector.

The governor and the city's mayor, by then Shirley Franklin, charged GDOT's and the city's planning chiefs, Paul Mullins and Mike Dobbins, to figure out a way to pay for the complex project. The result was a deal to move funding already budgeted for the replacement of the Spring Street viaduct across the Gulch downtown to provide the bulk of the funding

168

necessary for Fifth Street. This would provide some $11 million toward the $14 million project, the balance coming from Georgia Tech and other sources. Reaching clarity on the technical and financial direction, then, facilitated the bridge's reconstruction.

The awakening realization among students, faculty and staff that there were emerging reasons to cross over the bridge rather quickly picked up the pace from a trickle to floods of foot, cycle and Tech-provided transit traffic. Tech Square, then, became lined with food offerings and the Barnes and Noble campus bookstore, framed by the rehabbed classic Biltmore and Kim King's Centergy One building, home of Tech's Enterprise Innovation Institute. Served by the Tech Trolley connecting the Midtown MARTA station through the square to the campus, Tech Square transformed an urban wasteland into an urban delight. Thus, the Fifth Street Bridge became a park, indeed a quiet park, creating previously unthinkable connectivity and interactive synergy with Midtown.

Long story short, the probe into seeking Midtown connections resulted in the development of Tech Square, now a national model for joining the academy, Midtown, the city and the private sector into a rich mix of partnerships. The burbling up of activity and energy, plus Tech's obvious business supportive assets, led technology and business start-ups and

Fifth Street Bridge, replacing a utilitarian bridge with a seamless park, essential for connecting Georgia Tech with Midtown. *Jeb Dobbins.*

Soon after Shirley Franklin took office in 2002, she participated in a session of the Mayors Institute on City Design in La Jolla, California, where the topic she brought to share for discussion with a few other mayors and urban design experts was bridges. She wanted to investigate others' ideas for how to use Atlanta's bridges to better foster connectivity, to knit the city together.

related development to come forth, first modest and then robust and continuing.

The paths to these achievements, like any substantial redevelopment initiative, were complicated and ultimately depended on trusting relationships between the city, the state, GDOT, Midtown Alliance, Georgia Tech, private developers and the neighborhoods, represented by NPU E. These entities, interacting continuously, carried out their respective tasks to the mutual benefit of each. Still at this point encouraging reinvestment, the city managed the approval processes, indeed anticipating and leading the overall Midtown rezoning that followed.

Now, with Opportunity Zone incentives available west from West Peachtree Street, a veritable surge of high-rise commercial space is blossoming. Norfolk Southern Railways relocated its national headquarters from Norfolk. NCR established its national headquarters here, and Anthem, the insurance giant, built its Information Technology Center here. Completing this remarkable march of high-rise towers are CODA, Georgia Tech's high-performance computing center, and two or three student living structures. Regrettably, the city, the Midtown Alliance and Georgia Tech have not seized the opportunities provided through these massive and publicly supported investments to address any social needs, like developing housing that workers in these complexes can afford.

Other bridges further facilitated Midtown's linkages with what was becoming a burgeoning development bonanza west of the Connector. The Fourteenth Street bridge replacement project responded to the growing travel demand across the Connector with by then ever-growing Midtown growth and the early stages of the West Midtown renaissance. GDOT's starting point with the project, as with all of its big infrastructure projects, focused on moving cars, anticipating ongoing car growth and getting the job done within standard highway design requirements. From Midtown's perspective, though, the project offered the opportunity to grace the bridge with an impressive entry experience into Midtown, much like what had been achieved at Fifth Street. Its membership and its board were showing little progress in gaining traction on this more comprehensive vision. The GDOT project was moving along briskly through its design completion process toward bid documents.

The Midtown Alliance enlisted the city for its support, and the city's Chief Operating Officer, Lynette Young, along with Dobbins, met with the governor's office to review the project's status, Midtown's vision and the city's support for a better bridge. In spite of the about-to-happen status of the project, the governor's chief of staff at the time instructed GDOT to back off, look for appropriate enhancements and carry the result forward. The outcome was to shed one travel lane each way, replacing them with landscaped median splits, creating lighting, landscaping and graphic enhancements, designed by landscape architect Peter Drey, for the widened pedestrian ways and altogether snatch excitement out of what was an about to occur as yet another drab, ho-hum, car bridge.

Atlantic Station

The city's commitment to sound planning principles and the central role of planning and partnership in development practices continued to carry forward in the city's now expanding responses to development initiatives. Atlantic Station is an exemplar of this commitment. Located across the Downtown Connector from the Arts Center MARTA station area, the 123-acre site had lain fallow for twenty years as the defunct Atlantic Steel factory, a major brownfield site. Ideas for its redevelopment had been floated for some years, and in fact, it had been considered as a possible location for the Olympic stadium.

In 1996, soon after the Olympics ended, the aforementioned Charles Brown, an innovative and successful developer of suburban-style office parks, began to put the project together. His proposal called for over one million square feet of retail, six million square feet of office space and some five thousand units of housing. The initial concept projected a suburbanesque separation of the uses, all with prominently visible parking fields as the connective fabric and its sole point of access being off of Northside Drive to the west.

The city, with its overall policy of support for new investment, was keen to see the property redeveloped but had serious concerns about its nature and its access. The back-and-forth preliminary review process, all occasioned by the need for the property to be rezoned, led to a much more urban integration of the project's mixes of development type. In addition, the city was clear that relying solely on Northside Drive for access to a project of such magnitude, generating multiple thousands of trips, would require access from Midtown—in other words, a bridge crossing the Connector. This evolved into yet another Midtown bridge and connection to the Midtown MARTA station, the Seventeenth Street Bridge.

The project needed to overcome the complications of a 1998 prohibition to using federal transportation funds for the use of building capacity-expanding roads and bridges. EPA had placed this bar on the region due to the region's air quality conformity noncompliance. The developer and the city crafted a strategy that would argue the case for an exception. This project was to be a mixed-use development—that is, providing a pretty fair balance of housing, jobs and shopping on a single site, close to Midtown and the Arts Center MARTA station. Would not such a development improve regional air quality by shortening trip generation and trip lengths as compared with the predictable spread-out development patterns that characterized regional growth at the time?

The EPA held the whip hand in determining the validity and feasibility of that approach and, to its credit, determined through intense research that the argument was compelling. The agency not only greenlit the project but also worked with the various partners to designate it under the Project XL program as a national model for redressing environmentally unsound development practices. Beyond that, EPA lauded the project's commitment, a requirement under the prospective zoning, to remediate the extensive ground pollution under the old steel manufactory.

Moving forward, the nature of the bridge design as proposed by GDOT's urban design engineer, Joe Palladi, raised a number of red flags for the developer, the city and the EPA. Grounded in the same kind of car-dominated inertia described in earlier bridge projects, GDOT's initial proposals called for a wider, higher speed bridge, no pedestrian amenities, standard cobra-head lighting, all in all a totally car-dominated vision. Through back and forths on the issues, ultimately, Tom Coleman, the GDOT commissioner, called for significant modifications to its initial design, including narrowing it by one lane each way and allocating an additional $1 million for better design features.

Even at this point, getting the project done was a daunting task, involving the city's planning and public works departments, GDOT, the EPA, the Federal Highway Administration (FHWA), the ARC, other agencies needing to be in the loop and, of course, the developer. Governor Barnes called on the Georgia Regional Transportation Authority (GRTA) under Catherine

Atlantic Station, an intensifying mixed-use center looking from west to east toward Midtown. *Gene Phillips Photography.*

Ross's direction to convene what he called a "Greenlights" committee. All the agencies had their own priorities with multiple projects and responsibilities already in their hoppers, and their purpose here was to dedicate their principal staff's priorities to expedite implementation. The group met regularly, set tasks for all participants, identified any cross-jurisdictional or other technical obstacles, set deadlines for task completion and insisted on accountability from all. Without this discipline, it's hard to imagine a project of such magnitude getting done so quickly.

Meanwhile, the city and the Atlanta Development Authority worked with the developer to create a Tax Allocation District to defray much of the cost of public-serving improvements, mainly streets and parking. The ensuing development agreement underpinned the spirit and the letter of the zoning and other approvals. In addition, the agreement set first source hiring goals and insisted that 20 percent of the residential units would be available for families at 80 percent or below of the area median income.

By virtue of the developers' commitments to listen to community guidance, to interact positively with all of the levels of government whose approval would be necessary, then to continuously adjust their plans accordingly, difficult though it may have seemed, the massive project actually proceeded in a remarkably short time. Brown visited the city planning offices first in late 1996, and by 2003, the first offices, retail spaces and housing began to be occupied. The bridge opened in early 2004.

EASTSIDE

The Olympic Ripple Spreads East

Coinciding with the onrush of the Games, development activity east of the Old Fourth Ward was coming to life. Lower land costs, available sites and older industrial buildings were in good supply for retrofitting, and changing markets of younger people wanting to move in seemed promising. A major boost and consolidation of the area's attraction came with the transformation of GDOT's proposed freeway through the middle of the neighborhoods into Freedom Park.

Council District 2 Planning Study

As in the Olympic Ring, loft conversions began to repurpose and replace derelict light industrial buildings into residential and arts-oriented uses. Symbolic among these, Jane Fonda moved into one of the repurposed buildings on John Wesley Dobbs Avenue in 1996. By 1998, ideas had popped up among developers that challenged the city, the neighborhoods and the District 2 councilperson, Debbie Starnes, to pay attention. With the planning department, she wanted to seek ways where such dramatic shifts could respond to neighborhood concerns and take advantage of new investment in a city still not confident that investment was coming back into core and neglected areas.

Two project proposals prompted the need for a guiding planning framework to shape them in ways that complemented their settings and met their investors' needs. One was the replacement of the Central Metals recycling operation on the south side of North Highland Avenue, just east of the rail corridor that would later become the BeltLine. Here, a Gwinnett County suburban developer thought to venture into the nascent "urban" market. The other, on the other side of the rail line, also south of North

Starting in 1999, industrial properties redeveloping as mixed-use, here Highland Walk in the foreground and Inman Park Village beyond, followed in between by the 2012 opening of the BeltLine Eastside Trail. *Jeb Dobbins.*

Highland, was the proposed redevelopment of the newly fallow Mead Paper Company facilities into a new mixed-use development. Starnes's district included both, each however in a different NPU, with not necessarily complementary views. With a larger scale framework plan developed by the planning department, Starnes was able to negotiate through the thickets of neighborhood concern and investors' anxieties to enable the two planned and neighborhood responsive projects to go forward in 2000, setting the course for the Eastside's now ongoing growth spurts.

The BeltLine

When it went all-in for the BeltLine, the city did not just effectively kill off the MMPT and forestall bridging the Gulch, it discarded other development options as well. The Comprehensive Development Plan called for prioritizing city resources to strengthen existing concentrations of development along major travel corridors and in smaller centers throughout the city. Following that path, improving transit would have served unmet travel needs and boosted the incremental upgrading and densifying of already existing shopping and service corridors. It would have built ridership by serving established commuter routes. Lost, too, as seems inevitable now with the current City Gulch plan, is the realization of a downtown multimodal passenger terminal.

The BeltLine project emerged out of its CODA antecedents and the Georgia Tech architectural thesis of Ryan Gravel. His thesis advisor was Randy Roark, who, with others, as has been described in earlier chapters, had been working on such a project in the years leading up to the Olympics. Gravel added the idea of a twenty-two-mile streetcar loop to the project, not to serve any existing transit need but rather to open up new development on underused and abandoned industrial properties along the rail lines, away from the core city and existing commercial corridors. Through a compelling presentation of the project to private and city leaders, he began to build support for carrying it forward. The BeltLine concept got a pivotal boost through Council President Cathy Woolard's passionate advocacy, making full use of her considerable messaging and political organizing prowess. She saw the potential for a political trifecta: tantalizing development prospects, parks and trails and streetcars.

The project then proceeded along a path that included adding detail and securing funding. Ed McBrayer of the PATH Foundation brought to

Woolard's attention the importance of the project's rails-to-trails potential, like projects he was already implementing. He and Alycen Whiddon of the planning department had been advocating acting on that potential for some years, as described generally in the city's Parks, Open Space and Greenway Trails plan of 1993.

The Trust for Public Land, already working with the city planning department on securing conservation easements and titles to lands fronting the Chattahoochee River, commissioned a study for a more robust parks component for the project. Alex Garvin, a New York City urbanist, created the parks component for the growing concept that included a number of promising opportunity sites, the most dramatic of which was incorporating the Bellwood quarry in northwest Atlanta, operated by Vulcan Materials. This prospective park, over three hundred acres, would connect to Proctor Creek and be centered on the quarry, which would become a lake. The city's Department of Watershed Management, concerned about its existing lack of backup storage capacity, bought the quarry as a backup supply. The lake itself, then, would not be accessible for park users but could be a great scenic asset.

By then, the BeltLine project described itself as a development corridor with twenty-two miles of streetcars, parks and trails, thirty-six thousand housing units, generating thirty thousand permanent and temporary jobs. As noted above, the BeltLine's purpose was to open up new lands for development. In so doing it strayed far from Maynard Jackson's and then Bill Campbell's emphasis on programs aimed at addressing people's immediate needs, and especially those whose needs were greater. The streetcar ring did not connect to existing concentrations of jobs, services, housing, entertainment, hotel and other highly sought destinations. These were mainly located in Downtown, Midtown, Buckhead and the airport, where most people needed to travel to and from and where most of the city's support infrastructure, centering on MARTA rail, was already in place.

By this time, Mayor Franklin had given the responsibility for managing the project to the Atlanta Development Authority (ADA). In 2004, ADA commissioned a feasibility study to test the project's overall feasibility. The overall study came up positive.

In 2005, Tina Arbes of ADA asked Catherine Ross, by now back at Georgia Tech from her role as executive director of the Georgia Regional Transportation Authority (GRTA), to convene a panel to test the feasibility of the streetcar concept. With Ross as the chair, the panel included Bill Millar, president of the American Public Transit Association;

The study's consultant was heard to say that "of course we'll find it to be feasible," looking to follow-on work.

Tim Jackson, a principle of Glatting Jackson, a large transportation planning and engineering consultancy; and two Georgia Tech professors, Mike Meyer from civil engineering and Mike Dobbins from city planning.

The study raised a number of fundamental concerns about the project's transit feasibility. Since it didn't connect to where most people's destinations were located, the panel noted that the streetcar as proposed would not serve existing travel needs and thus would likely generate little ridership. It questioned the seeming chicken and egg question: that it would take many years and lots of money to build before it would attract enough investment to eventually generate ridership. Could not the $3 or $4 billion cost to build it be better used to meet the transit needs of the existing populations? There were a number of other questions that seemed to dim its feasibility, like that it wasn't a continuous loop in fact but instead several disconnected segments, as well as a number of other difficult technical challenges. The project's boosters, however, discounted these cautionary notes.

Woolard had figured out that the most promising revenue source and funding stream would be to create a Tax Allocation District as by then the council had put in place Downtown and for Atlantic Station. Her first priority interest in the project was the northeast quadrant, her former council district. That area, relatively affluent, seemed best primed for boosting development and had already been experiencing considerable new investment in older, obsolescent industrial properties along the unused rail. In addition, the BeltLine could prevent the use of that corridor for the projected commuter rail line to Athens, a project vehemently opposed by the area's residents. Yet a TAD for that generally well-off area would not qualify under the state redevelopment powers act. To qualify, the TAD would have to serve a majority of low-wealth neighborhoods, so the decision was made to include the whole of the project's trajectory. Most of those neighborhoods' demographics, like poverty, unemployment and disinvestment, would qualify the project for TAD funding.

As the council was taking up the proposed TAD ordinance in 1995, community activists were raising concerns about what the project would do to meet real needs of real people, not just for improving transit service but more particularly providing for affordable housing, by then already a growing concern. While the BeltLine advocates resisted this objection,

Deborah Scott, founding executive director of newly formed Georgia Stand-Up, Andy Schneggenburger and Kate Little of Atlanta Housing Association of Neighborhood-based Developers (AHAND) and others succeeded in getting provisions to meet their concerns into the ordinance. These stipulated the use of some of the funds to create affordable housing, aiming at 5,600 units of the 36,000-unit total the BeltLine was projecting. Scott was also able to insert provisions for a Community Benefits Agreement—that is, an effort to stipulate outcomes for various other aspects of the program aimed at providing jobs, improving equity in its use of funds, and as a means to hold the agency accountable. Despite concerns raised along the way by citizens and the city council, most of the issues related to housing, jobs and equity remain unfulfilled.

Against this background, the city council voted to approve the TAD. In so doing, the project depleted all of the city's remaining access to the TAD funding resource, which is limited to 10 percent of the city's overall tax digest. The funding enabled the formation of Atlanta BeltLine Inc., spinning out from the Atlanta Development Authority. In the same time frame, reflecting the allure of the idea, the nonprofit Atlanta BeltLine Partnership formed as a way to seek private sector and foundation philanthropy to support the mission.

Emerging out of the TAD approval, with its city council–imposed stipulation for affordable housing, came the contradiction of creating a tax-funded revenue stream that depended on raising property and land values, thus taxes, even as the biggest obstacle to providing affordable housing is land cost. Thus the ability to write down land costs had been flummoxed by the aim for the ever higher land values that fuel the BeltLine's coffers.

Always posed as "the solution," the BeltLine streetcar loop over the next five years resisted any voicing of concerns about the loop not getting people to where they needed to go. Finally, beginning at about the time that the city received an American Recovery and Reinvestment Act grant in 2010 to build the piece of streetcar connecting Centennial Olympic Park to the King Center, the agency decided to go all in with streetcars. It got support from the city council to become the city's transit planning agency, whereupon it projected thirty more miles of streetcars, now totaling fifty-two miles, that would finally connect the ring east–west to where destinations were actually concentrated, in Downtown and Midtown. The council adopted this plan. At this point, then, the city was funding three transit agencies:

- MARTA, the city's transit workhorse and the only agency with any experience and tested competence
- the city's own Downtown Streetcar, which it created, built and operated, usually running empty, to cover the mile and a half distance between Centennial Olympic Park and the King Center, until MARTA took it over in 2017
- and the BeltLine, which had no experience in building or operating any transit service

One of the most intriguing aspects of the BeltLine phenomenon, very Atlanta, has been its ability to capture the imagination of so many Atlantans. Indeed, its success in projecting itself, repeatedly trumpeting its superlatives, has become a national symbol for Atlanta. Beginning with Gravel's thesis, whose presentation graphics were brilliant, followed by waves of top-of-the-line urban design and image management consultants, the organization continues to project compelling graphic representations and a robust marketing presence. The results are impressive, with major developments multiplying on the east side, most using the BeltLine tagline as their come-on. On the west side, though on a modest scale, development is raising ever greater concerns about gentrification and displacement among long-term mostly low-wealth and African American citizens.

As of this writing in late 2019, the organization maintains its high profile, achieving the kind of prominence that has provided it political cover. With a staff of about thirty, of whom about ten are director level or higher, the organization has carved out its space in the city as its own bureaucracy, a kind of alternate city inside the city. It has expended about $700 million, the majority of it in the more affluent eastside, displacing people faced with the growing tax burden that is the core of the BeltLine's revenue stream. Along the way, it has managed to resist occasional citizen pushback against the speculation, dislocation and otherwise inequitable impact it has visited on the low-wealth neighborhoods through which the streetcar is planned to pass.

According to its November 2019 website, over its first fifteen years, or about 60 percent of its funding life, the BeltLine scorecard lists its program elements along with what it has actually delivered for each:

- 33 miles of trails—it has delivered about 10, with more underway
- 5,600 units of affordable housing out of an original projected total of 36,000 new units—it has delivered about 1,500 units, many with others' funding and development resources
- 1,300 acres of new greenspace—it has delivered about 400 acres and has more in the works
- 1,100 acres of environmental cleanup—it has delivered about 400 acres
- 46 miles of streetscape improvements—it has delivered about 2 miles
- 22 miles of transit—it has delivered no transit
- And a whole lot of art and other popular cultural events

In sum, the BeltLine has created a very popular amenity with its eastside trail. It has provided great exposure and support for dozens of artists. It produces popular events. It has developed a few parks. Most dramatic among these is Old Fourth Ward Park, where planners, building on what water quality advocate Bill Eisenhower had proposed twenty-five years earlier, used an existing spring and pesky storm water flooding events to create a lake as its centerpiece. The BeltLine's allure has greatly boosted property values and taxes, thus its revenue stream. It has created multiple plans and sub-area plans of one kind and another, covering land use, zoning, urban design, trails and streetcars. Always insisting that the streetcar ring must be the baseline given, it has engaged citizens in contemplating what transit futures might look like around the ring.

In so doing, however, the project has diverted city resources away from its areas of greatest need, indeed perpetrating the dislocation of lower wealth citizens from their homes and small businesses from affordable locations. These outcomes run counter to the city's stated equity aspirations. As a transit project, as suggested in the transit feasibility report of 2005 and the BeltLine's own report card, its future remains unresolved. With its high cost (the lion's share of the BeltLine's overall budget), lack of funding sources, required delivery timelines, geometric and other technical obstacles, rapidly changing transportation technologies and choices, and lack of projected ridership make rail transit an ever more distant longshot.

BUCKHEAD

The Olympics effects were less pronounced in Buckhead, the wealthy north sector of the city. Buckhead had maintained healthy growth and investment strength even as the rest of the city had been languishing over the twenty years or so leading up to the Games. At the time, the neighborhoods that make up northeast Buckhead, all in NPU-B, were active in seeking to rein in some of the negative effects of the area's explosive growth. Issues of needing a fair and workable planning framework, land use compatibility, parking and transportation impacts and neighborhood conservation set up lively and not always friendly NPU meetings. What had become different over that period was the rise of the planning department's and the city's activism to try to redirect the negative consequences of the unplanned, one-off patterns of the area's land development processes.

Extending the momentum of post-Olympic support for planning principles, the city applied the Comprehensive Development Plan, zoning and transportation planning tools to bear in its project review and approval processes, generally improving on the initial proposals. The city's aim was to balance the competing interests of one-off projects into a guiding, holistic, citizen-involved and connective framework for decision-making. A signal planning success was validation of the Comprehensive Development Plan as the guiding policy for dealing with zoning changes. The city had denied a zoning change application for a mega project north of Lenox Square on the grounds of noncompliance with the CDP. The developer successfully challenged the denial in lower court, but that decision was overturned on appeal, a city appeal that was supported by citizen-generated friends of the court briefs, and the project died. The recognition by the courts that the CDP may trump earlier "higher and best use" developer-driven rationales had ripple effects into the future for balancing community values bedded in the CDP with development practices.

THE AGENCIES

The city's Olympic and post-Olympic activities involved a number of rolling partnerships with other agencies beyond ACOG, CODA, CAP and Midtown, many of which played crucial roles in one or another of development initiatives in the city. Here follows a snapshot of the activities of the many partnering agencies without whose participation and support little could have gone forward.

Atlanta Development Authority

Upon the mandated dissolution of CODA in 1997, its mission was subsumed into a public "superagency," the Atlanta Development Authority (ADA, now Invest Atlanta). The ADA consolidated five existing agencies into a single multipurpose authority that could take advantage of public-private development opportunities that had been part of many Olympics projects. The city created with ADA an informal "development council," stemming from a planning and development "sub-cabinet," set up by Mayor Campbell and Byron Marshall, his COO. For the purpose of coordinating information, plans and projects, this group brought together the major public and community development agencies for ongoing policy and project coordination. Co-chaired by the Commissioner of Planning and Community Development Dobbins and the Executive Director of the ADA, Kevin Hanna, the group met regularly during the post-Olympic years. The participants included planning, housing, public works and other city agencies, the Atlanta Housing Authority, Atlanta Public Schools, MARTA, the Atlanta Neighborhood Development Partnership led by Hattie Dorsey, HUD and other organizations related to the agenda of the day. This comprehensive and inclusive redevelopment approach among public and nonprofit agencies constituted an important, if not so visible, legacy of the organizational framework that carried off the Olympics. In the same period, the city began to make accelerating use of tax allocation districts, as described earlier, and the ADA took on the responsibility of managing the various TADs that were adopted through the years.

Atlanta Housing Authority

The Atlanta Housing Authority, already involved through the land deal that provided the new Olympic Village dormitory site, had been going through hard times coming into the acceleration of preparations for the Games. The housing authority had been on HUD's troubled list for some years, with poor service, rising deterioration and vacancy rates, mismanagement, cronyism, crime and questions about its finances. In an effort to turn the authority around, Mayor Bill Campbell tapped Renee Glover, a corporate attorney and an AHA board member at the time, to serve as its chair.

HUD had awarded the agency a rehab grant in 1993 for one of its most challenged complexes, Techwood/Clark Howell Homes, the nation's first public housing project, built in 1934. The 990-unit complex across the street from the under-construction Olympic Village occupied the lands separating Georgia Tech from Downtown. Reviewing the situation with an aggressive frame of mind, Glover decided instead to go for the first HOPE VI grant, a new HUD program managed by Secretary Andrew Cuomo aimed at deconcentrating poverty and redeveloping housing communities into mixed-income neighborhoods. Ultimately incorporating a complicated private-sector partnership with developer Egbert Perry of the Integral Group, the result was the first completed HOPE VI project in the nation, the first phase of which was nearing completion when the Olympics took place. The HOPE VI model stipulated and incentivized mixed-income outcomes—that is, that significant portions of the redeveloped complexes would be reserved for public housing eligible families, determined by income, and the balance would be available at a mix of below-market rate and full-market rate rents.

While public housing redevelopment under this model proved controversial to some because of both temporary and permanent dispersal of low-income families, AHA's record was remarkable in achieving mostly stable, mixed-income communities. In general, 40 percent of these units go to low-income people (public housing eligible), 20 percent to low-to-middle-income people (tax credit eligible) and 40 percent going at market rates. With only 40 percent of low-income people (or less, since reducing density was a HOPE VI goal as well) able to return, the authority provided Section 8 vouchers for those dispersed, allowing them—or obliging them—to find housing in neighborhoods around the region, with the voucher covering the difference between what they could afford and market rates.

The Authority and Integral completed the five planned phases of Centennial Place by 2003. The transformation achieved the lasting benefit of breaking down the physical and psychological barriers between Georgia Tech and Downtown. Georgia Tech staff, faculty and students joined in the mix of those moving into the new neighborhood, about 40 percent of whom were former residents. The neighborhood's children attend a highly rated elementary school supported by the combined resources of the Authority, Atlanta Public Schools, the YMCA and Georgia Tech.

Centennial Place, the first national use of HUD's HOPE VI program, replacing Techwood/Clark Howell Homes, the nation's first public housing project, with a new mixed-income community. *Jeb Dobbins.*

With success at Centennial Place, the authority moved steadily toward redeveloping several other public housing communities along similar lines. These included the East Lake Meadows, John Hope Homes, John Egan Homes and Harris Homes, these three ringing the AUC campuses, Capitol and Grady Homes east of Downtown, among others. This level of activity foundered in the Kasim Reid mayoralty, as the Authority lost its leadership, momentum and mission, leaving many of its former communities unoccupied and fallow.

Atlanta Regional Commission

The Atlanta Regional Commission (ARC) played a significant role in boosting planning consciousness and practice into its constituent jurisdictions, in which the city was a fully active participant. Most significant for the city and for the region was its role in orchestrating the way out of the air quality noncompliance ban on the use of federal funds for capacity-increasing highway projects. The ban resulted from a successful lawsuit brought in 1998 by the Southern Environmental Law Center, the Georgia Conservancy, the Sierra Club and the Southern Organizing Committee, among others. The EPA found the region and its Regional Development Plan to be exceeding air quality standards under the Clean Air Act. For a region thriving in its ever-outward development boom, the ban posed a huge rock in the road, and it reeled under its new national headline in the *Wall Street Journal* as the "poster child of sprawl." The EPA required the Atlanta region to re-model its growth patterns in such a way as to bring it back into compliance.

Through an intense and in-depth study of how to do that, the ARC, under the leadership of consultant Tom Weyandt, convened Atlanta's and the region's counties' major planning and transportation officials to noodle over what to do about the crisis. So went forward a lengthy process, using the agency's extensive air quality modeling capacity to test all alternative patterns and combinations to meet the requirements. The outcome that worked was to redirect 10 percent of anticipated growth into existing towns and urban centers and 10 percent away from projected greenfield development.

That seemingly simple policy shift basically reduced projected trip lengths and the corresponding auto emissions and attendant air pollutants to an acceptable level. The group came to recommend a voluntary, "carrot" approach, contingent on local jurisdictions acting to support more compact development codes and incentives, the origin of the Livable Centers Initiative program. As it happened, the ARC was the designated recipient of the USDOT's Congestion Management/Air Quality (CMAQ) funding stream. These funds, then, became the source for the "carrot" to induce jurisdictions to participate. Step one was incentivizing changes in local policy and plans to support more compact development as well as pedestrian, bike and transit-oriented improvements. Step two offered the opportunity to use CMAQ dollars for the capital funding necessary to begin to implement the plans developed in the planning stage. The proviso for use of these funds was to incorporate tangible policy shifts into local zoning and compatible transportation and other regulatory provisions governing development.

Atlanta, whose planners had played a major role in shaping the new policy and program, quickly put the program to use, first in Midtown, which had recently completed its Blueprints plan, where the city was in the process of rezoning the whole of the district in ways that supported the LCI goals. By 2003, the city had used the program to focus attention on several other areas of the city, many of them sparked by citizens' initiatives. ARC has designated some 120 other LCI zones, which have been instrumental in directing regional growth into centers of walkable, mostly medium-density town centers throughout the Atlanta region. The program has significantly altered the region's settlement patterns from sprawl to centers, ranging in size from villages, to commercial corridors, to urban centers.

MARTA

MARTA performed an outstanding job moving people during the Games. In an agreement with ACOG and GDOT, MARTA provided free ridership to all persons holding a ticket to any event during the Games. In preparation, the agency extended its North Line and added two more stations. It carried twenty-five million people over the seventeen days of formal Games events, way beyond normal usage. As a result, car traffic on the freeways pretty much avoided congestion.

On another front, taking advantage of the provisions of the Intermodal Surface Transportation Efficiency Act of 1991 (ISTEA), MARTA's general manager, Rick Simonetta, launched a Transit Oriented Development (TOD) program. The plan was to replace the five-thousand-car surface parking lot at the Lindbergh station, where the rail service splits into the north line and the northeast line. The idea of TOD was to actually build a mix of "origins" (houses) and "destinations" (jobs and shopping) at the stations. The intended transportation result was to reduce travel distances and concomitant automobile congestion. By now a no brainer, at the time it seemed novel and a bit edgy.

MARTA put together a request for proposals that seemed to anticipate suburban-style office parks as its intended result. The city, however, was able to inject a call for more integrated and urbanistic proposals into the mix. Only two development teams responded, one for a suburban-style swoopy streets lower density approach, and the other by Carter Development and ultimately Harold A. Dawson Company for a well-organized, mixed-use placemaking approach.

The city weighed in strongly in favor of the Carter proposal, citing not just its placemaking superiority but its all-in inclusion of minority development partners, and that team was selected. Never simple, though, the shifts in policy and zoning requirements necessary to implement the

Lindbergh City Center Transit Oriented Development, transforming a five-thousand-car parking lot above a MARTA station into a vibrant mixed-use community. *Jeb Dobbins*.

development were daunting. The city's commitment to carry out such initiatives with the participation of the affected neighborhoods led to an intensive mediation process. With sufficient neighborhood support, Lee Morris, the district council member, concurred, and the city approved the project's zoning requirements.

GDOT

Again conceptually led by CODA's streetscape work, the Capitol Avenue bridge modifications spanning I-20 to suitably connect downtown at the capitol to the Olympic stadium, encouraged GDOT to build the project. Overseen by GDOT bridge engineer Paul Liles and designed by architect Richard Rothman, the result was a well-landscaped gateway. This streetscape axis, punctuated by the Olympic sculpture tower and logo where Muhammad Ali opened the Games with the Olympic torch and flame, now provides the entry into GSU's south campus. The street (now called Hank Aaron Drive south of the freeway interchange) is now framing redevelopment of the site for the reuse of the stadium facilities for GSU as part of the ambitious Carter mixed-use development partnership described earlier.

Beyond its participation and support for the Hank Aaron Drive project, GDOT carried out welcoming interstate interchange landscaping improvements, transforming bleak and barren entry points into the core city into welcoming green gateways. These improvements, supported by federal funding under ISTEA for transportation enhancement activities, utterly changed the city's entry experience, and the department continues to maintain them in their now mature state. Little by little, the struggles on other projects notwithstanding, the department has increasingly addressed the market and popular demand for balancing its primary auto-serving culture with greater understanding for repurposing its right-of-way to accommodate transit, bikes, peds and streetscape priorities.

Summary

In the calculus of Olympic impact, then, was all this development going to happen anyway in these locations? Probably not, at least no time soon. Indeed, Centennial Olympic Park itself and the CODA streetscape achievements may have directed more of the shape, pace and quality of development for Downtown and the city than any other Olympic investment. Important in understanding this phenomenon is that it took the combined and interactive actions of the city government; its neighborhoods; its development authority, now called Invest Atlanta; Central Atlanta Progress; and a creative development community to make it happen. These forces worked together to create the plans and manage their implementation where connectivity was the key and enduring component. This emphasis on connectivity and interactivity was unusual for Atlanta, the quintessential "one-off" city.

We have given an overview of the city's planning, design and development policies and practices that framed the Olympics and then whose standards spread in the ensuing years. Aside from rebounding from the population and investment declines of the prior twenty-five years, several themes and questions emerge that characterize the Olympic jolt visited upon the city:

- the necessity of collaboration across historic divides—race, class, culture, public, private, citizenry—to get stuff done
- the opportunities, barriers and questions that remain out of this era of collaboration:
  o Moderating racism?
  o Narrowing the wealth divide?
  o Respecting government?

- o Recognizing the need for planning, development creativity and capability and channeling that toward greater than "one-off" purposes?
- the central involvement of city planning and urban design professionals in development policy, plans, design and processes
- the essential authority of city government and other public agencies to enable and to regulate development in the effort to work on behalf of and in service to their full constituencies

There are pros and cons that attach to all of these themes and questions. There is little doubt, however, that the city's and CODA's work joined the ACOG work in laying the foundation for the turnaround that occurred in the years following, measured in investment and population growth and aiming at greater equity and engagement among its citizens.

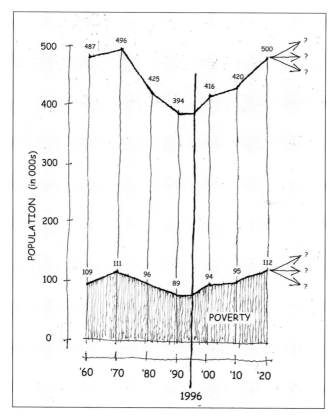

Whither next? Population trajectory from the Olympics to the present and the range of possible futures, showing the rise in the numbers of citizens living in poverty.

Regrettably, despite success by the many public-private partnerships spawned by the Olympic experience, the city in many ways seems to have reverted to its old "one-off" ways. Its wealth divide is growing. Its population living in poverty remains consistently in the 20 to 25 percent range, which means that even as population grows so too do the numbers of people living in poverty: there are now about twenty thousand more people living in poverty than during the Olympics. Children growing up in poverty have scant chance of escaping it. Even with a boom economy that tracks from the Olympics forward, Atlanta is losing its opportunity to leverage its strengths to redress its shames of race and class divisions. Planning as a policy and a process fell to marginal relevance. Lost was its utility as a tool for addressing these seemingly intractable obstacles to gaining greater equity for its citizens. Chapter 6 shares the authors' reflections on others' comments about the Games, characterizations of Atlanta, the "twin peaks" approach, the IOC's response and Atlanta's pivot back to the old ways.

6

REFLECTIONS

This book seeks to tell the rest of the story, covering realities and perceptions that are by and large missed in the literature and even in the memory of people who experienced this fifteen-year-long Olympic "moment." What the literature conveys is basically two pictures, neither particularly accurate or comprehensive. One view, tending to reflect the private sector perspective, is that ACOG did it all, and in spite of the city's involvement, the Olympic Games were great. The other, tending to reflect more academic and some media coverage, is narrowly focused on one or another aspect of the bigger story and so lacks context, sometimes even building on past inaccuracies.

For us, the rest of the story is bedded in the sustained presence of public, professional city planning guidance, a role that Mayor Jackson initiated and supported, a role that sustained through Mayor Campbell's administration. Planning was at the table across the span from conceptualization to design and implementation of the many projects that the city and its partners undertook, from 1990 into the early 2000s.

The larger backdrop for these public policy and implementation shifts was the deadline-driven collaborations between public and private and accordingly greater accommodations between Black and white cultures. Out of these messy and uneven democratic processes, with a conscious effort to carry out the work inclusively and transparently, came a reset on how Atlantans saw themselves. Not only did physical transformations begin to appear, but also cultural diversity found more comfortable places in the flow of city life.

THE ONGOING INTERACTION BETWEEN ATLANTA'S HYPE AND ITS TRASH-TALK

Long known for "hype and pride" (which *AJC* analyst Bert Roughton has called "The Hubris Thing"), often blinding itself to the realities of messy American urbanity, Atlanta nevertheless has propelled itself forward, sometimes naively, sometimes intentionally, often with astonishing results, but also with persistent disappointments. Quite possibly, without the "hubris thing" Atlanta would never have even considered the challenge of hosting the 1996 Olympic Games. Interestingly, the hubris thing has also often blinded Atlanta commentators to the point of unrealistically "trashing" its many challenges. This dynamic causes many to forget that going into as well as coming out of the Olympics Atlanta was best known for its civil rights struggles, both successes and ongoing obstacles. More immediately the region had been dubbed as the poster child for sprawl, with poor air quality, gridlocked traffic congestion and a lack of walkable urban amenities.

In the context of its Olympics adventure, commentators projected Atlanta's image and identity along three tracks:

First, both the local and international press lamented the absence of a cutting-edge architectural icon that could symbolize the Games in a single bold stroke. *Architectural Record*, for example, dubbed it the "No Frills, No Thrills" Olympics. This perspective reflected the all-in critical acceptance of the notion that only international trophy architects could properly express the imageability of such an event, to exalt the elites embodied in the IOC, with their exorbitant cost implications noted in chapter 4. Related, and generally accurate at the time, was the lament of the city's lack of easily accessible and abundant amenities. In hindsight, Centennial Park perhaps has come to fill both roles in an uncharacteristically modest way, not so flashy but with the right stuff in the right place, with real contributions to the city's physical and social fabric and a sense of urban identity for visitor and citizen alike.

Second, there was a lot of criticism from the international press for temporarily failed systems, like a couple of days of glitches with IBM's computer system and a bus system that used buses from all over the country, thus drivers unfamiliar with Atlanta's travel networks. Some of these criticisms were partially on point. But others may have been accountable to ACOG's miscalculation in leaving out the media in its housing strategies, instead favoring accommodating the elites close in. This resulted in the media's lodgings being dispersed around the city and region—not a wise move.

Third, rereading the local accounts and assessments from 1997 on, particularly from the academic community, one is struck by the narrowness of topics selected for analysis and assessment. Much of this work pointed out issues legitimately ripe for criticism, yet usually lacking the broader context from which the issues arose. These analyses also tend not to describe how and why choices were made and how they may have been addressed differently. While this is not unusual in academic research, understanding the fullness of the Olympics' impact on the city would seem to be necessary to assess and make use of the value of the research findings. Unfortunately, too, errors in some of these accounts have been picked up by subsequent researchers as givens, baseless though they are. A prime example has been the occasional representation that the purchase and construction of Centennial Olympic Park displaced thousands of low-wealth residents. In fact, there was no pre-existing residential population on the site, the error apparently stemming from confusing the park site with a public housing project lying a half mile to the north (a whole different story covered in chapter 5).

THE EXPECTATIONS OF THE "UNEASY ALLIANCE"

Preparations for the Olympics mostly played to two local audiences at opposite ends of the spectrum, matching the two historic faces of Atlanta. Atlanta is a city with a longstanding albeit uneasy alliance between the city's business leadership, mostly white, and its post-1973 African American political leaders, many of whom were associated with the city's enviable record of civil rights advances. Race relations, therefore, are always present in any contemplated initiative.

This alliance, dubbed by Andy Young as the "Atlanta Way," has produced many ameliorating successes, though race and class relations persist and the alliance has done little to lift low-wealth citizens out of the poverty trap. Mayor Jackson's "Twin Peaks of Mt Olympus" aptly and with poetic irony captured this baseline Atlanta reality—ACOG seeing the Games as the mother of all business marketing opportunities and the mayor seeing a chance to significantly tackle the socioeconomic problems accrued over many years. The twin peaks characterization at the time represented places that Olympic host cities didn't want to go. Most host cities focused mainly on elaborate sports venues and a few carefully chosen redevelopment projects, mostly gathered in "safe and secure" zones easy to manage. In Atlanta, the two "peaks" represented a framing vision, which moved the city forward, while certainly not altogether meeting its lofty expectations. There were no trophy architect-designed iconic venues, and neither did the inner city get fixed in six years. Since the Atlanta Games, though, the IOC has echoed Atlanta's dual commitment, gradually incorporating and now emphasizing to bidders the importance of a more socially inclusive and economically conscious approach. This showed, for example, in the London Games, where Atlanta labor leader Stuart Acuff played a consulting role.

THE IOC AND THE "MOST EXCEPTIONAL" OLYMPICS

Many Atlantans, particularly those in the business community and local media, wrung their hands over Juan Antonio Samaranch's characterization of the Atlanta Games as the "most exceptional." His usual unrestrained post-Olympic accolade had always been "the best Games ever." The longtime IOC czar and the ruling IOC European elite seemed to have a hard time accepting that Atlanta, a small, mostly Black and poor city, had won the Olympics. Whatever was going to happen during the Games, this underlying cynicism was bound to influence any assessments.

As noted above, though, since Atlanta the IOC has broadened and strengthened its emphasis on host cities' commitment to legacies beyond its venues, incorporating measures like Mayor Jackson initiated. On the other hand, its leaders have demanded a more manageable, predictable, accountable, top-down, single point of contact authority to manage the whole process, In retrospect, we wonder if Atlanta's very messiness, with diverse portals of access, resulted in a process more responsive to everyday citizens.

Fitting the ACOG initiatives into a larger connectivity framework, utilizing the existing Comprehensive Development Plan to create the Olympic Development Program, running the choices through the NPU advisory structure, and finally CODA focusing those efforts into concrete planning and development strategies for nearby neighborhoods, while not perfect, seems to have worked for a broader cross-section of citizens. ACOG, which limited its interests to the venues and the aspirations of the business community, did not like this peak of the Olympic effort, yet was obliged to pay attention and ultimately, however grudgingly, respect it. As always in Atlanta, though gradually and unevenly improving, race and class dominated the attitudes embedded in the twin peaks.

Host cities for the Olympics should expect their Games, and both the positive and the negative energy generated by the preparation, the event itself and the aftermath to make the realities that constitute the heart and soul of a city hyper-visible. There is no real way to hide flaws or change a century of racism, layered in social, cultural and white-dominated attitudes toward government in six years and afterward. Thus for Atlanta, the Olympics continue as a mirror reflecting the past, in which one hopes that its lessons will brighten its window into the future.

Overall, a lot was done to turn around Atlanta's long, slow slide. The confluence of an absolute deadline, major new facilities, a widespread upgrade of streetscapes and parks, market shifts toward in-town living and boosting support for neighborhood-based community development corporations are stories that both the local and international press, as well as academic research, have largely missed—this more interesting "real story."

ATLANTA'S PIVOT BACK TO THE OLD WAYS

By any comprehensive measure, the Olympic period generated many positives, both leading up to and then following the events themselves. Some of these are directly attributable to the Games, some more coincidental but catalyzed by the time deadlines and still others reflecting market shifts.

Some of Atlanta's most intractable challenges, however, persist. As noted in chapter 5, the city ranks at the bottom of the GINI Index, which measures the wealth divide. Of the one hundred thousand people gained since the Olympics, twenty thousand more Atlantans live in poverty than in 1996. And a recent Harvard-Berkeley study concluded that Atlanta's kids growing up in poverty have but a 4 percent chance of escaping it. Remember that the Renaissance Policy Board goals in 1997 included an "attack on poverty," boosting public education and improved access to jobs, particularly for those without cars.

Though easing somewhat, racism still plays a significant role in how things are done in Atlanta. Since the subsidence of the Olympic era, from the early 2000s, business and political leadership until recently has shown no sustained commitment to improve housing affordability and other conditions of inequity that mainly affect African American communities.

After thirty years of trying, though, the message of the need to stem rising housing costs brought by the Regional Housing Forum has finally spread into the mainstream. Stalwarts Bill Bolling, Bruce Gunter, the Atlanta Neighborhood Development Partnership and many others have joined in ever more effective partnerships to press for housing affordability. With poverty spreading regionally, the effort has now fully engaged the Atlanta Regional Commission. The issue was front and center in the 2017 mayoral campaign. The eventual winner, Keisha Lance Bottoms, promised raising $1 billion of funding support, though without a strategy for attaining such a goal. Yet little by little the city has begun to introduce affordability into its approval and resource support processes.

Coming out of the Olympics, the city had pivotal choices for responding to growing development forces. It could prioritize connectivity in transportation, housing and job access and rebalance its policy and resource commitments toward greater support for its impoverished neighborhoods. Or it could revert to Atlanta's tradition of boosting one-off projects. The Olympics themselves were conceived and started out in this tradition. Only Mayor Jackson's vision and his Olympic Development Program spread the project to full citywide relevance. The city instead seems to have opted for the one-off project approach and in so doing reasserted policy support for the initiatives of the haves over the have-nots, whether intentionally or not. The shame is that city and private investment ventures that adjoin these neighborhoods, really big-ticket projects with lots of government subsidy, have had the opportunity through community benefit agreements to step up and address some neighborhood-identified needs.

One positive note to support neighborhood-engaged planning, though, did arise through community activism around the Falcons stadium project. While the stadium further walled off Vine City and English Avenue from connecting to downtown, the philanthropically constituted Westside Futures Fund through regular forums, has responded to some of neighborhood-identified needs and priorities and begun to support and build projects accordingly. This kind of commitment in some ways reflects the linkages formed for the Olympics, modest as they are, given the enormity of the divide.

More broadly, sound planning, while uneven and contested at times, was key to making the Olympics work in a way that by and large left the city better off than before. Public and private leadership, though not always on the same page, sought and maintained an inclusive, comprehensive, cross-interest, cross-disciplinary and communicative process that guided making decisions. The urgency of meeting the absolute deadline bound people together to adopt common goals and implementation strategies.

Without the city's Olympic Development Program, without the Comprehensive Development Plan it was based on, would the city have been able to advance Mayor Jackson's vision of the twin peaks? Like much of the complicated dynamics that produced the event, it is difficult to declare causality, to separate cause from coincidence, from chance, from serendipity. Yet reviewing Atlanta's more traditional lurch from project to project without the connectivity and balance that planning provides, planning can claim some credit for the positive effects that the Olympics surely achieved.

Support for maintaining the productive nexus between planning, design and development forces and private, public and community forces, declined over the next several years. Planning was not at the table as development and resource decisions got made. For lack of acknowledgement and support from the top, planning reverted to its mainly paper-pushing zoning and permitting functions, reacting to development pressures rather than shaping them. This drift frustrated planning staff members who had experienced times of greater respect and involvement in the big-picture issues where their expertise and their voice would have produced better outcomes.

Along with the erosion of a planning presence in the affairs of the city's development, the Neighborhood Planning Unit system has been losing the voice and the city resources that it had during the Olympic period. Over the years since, the growing centralization and opacity of major city decisions has been dismissing the role of neighborhoods and its CDCs. Presently, there is movement afoot, under the umbrella of the community-building Center for Civic Innovation, to develop strategies for regaining and respecting the decentralized neighborhood voice in the affairs of the city. The city, too, seems to be rethinking its support in positive ways. At a most basic level, a city is its people and its neighborhoods, who ultimately judge whether things are getting better or worse for all.

On a more positive note, the Quality of Life zoning tools put in place in the wake of the Olympics have become rules of choice for many new developments citywide, modified from time to time as community values, conditions and market responses desire. In the face of growing recognition of the threats of climate change, the city developed first-rate Climate Action and Resiliency Plans that hopefully will guide better-informed and connected decision-making across a range of issues. In the same vein, overcoming some private property owners' concerns, the city has succeeded in launching a Better Buildings Challenge program, taking steps to mitigate rooftops' heat island effects and to keep track of water and energy use, to the benefit of building owners' operation and maintenance costs and to improve air quality and water conservation. And the City Planning Department has produced "The Atlanta City Design, Aspiring to the Beloved Community," a vision piece that seeks to craft a future embodying the values of equity, nature, progress, access and ambition.

CONCLUSION

Atlanta's Olympic moment represents a major milestone in Atlanta's development progression. It either catalyzed or coincided with major shifts in the marketplace, where in-town living, environmental sustainability, choice in living and working environments, choice in travel modes and appreciation for more compact and diverse communities all came together. It cracked the door open on the visible and growing needs of its low-wealth communities, beginning to listen, to touch the surface of poverty with job, housing and neighborhood revitalization commitments. Using the Olympics opportunity, the city and its private sector adopted new policies, plans, urban design and projects to respond to and further stimulate the new city building partnerships to benefit all its citizens, not perfect, but a start. Atlanta is teeming with life and civic amenities and just may become a city for all.

APPENDIX

Urban Park Development in the Olympic Ring (from 1990 to 2010, investments in millions of dollars)			
Park	**Acreage**	**Investment 1990–1996**	**Investment 1996–2008**
Freedom Park	210	1.0	**n.a.**
Piedmont Park	230	2.0	$62
Grant Park	150	**n.a.**	**n.a.**
Centennial Park	20	28	15
Woodruff Park	4	6.0	0
Total	**614**	**37+**	**77+**

Notes: acreages contain both existing and new parkland

Source: compiled by authors

TABLE 3

ACOG Olympic Budget	Amount (millions of dollars)
Revenues	
TV Broadcast Rights	559.50
Joint Venture (ACOG & USOC)	462.50
National Sponsorships, Licensing, Olympic Coin Sales	
International Sponsorships	77.60
Ticket Sales	422.00
Other Revenue:	151.60
Interest Income, Ticket Service Charge, Accommodation Fees, Olympic License Tags, Olympic Brick Program	
Merchandise	32.00
Expenditures	
Administration	196.37
Construction: Venues, Olympic Village, Centennial Park	532.73
Operations	946.10
Contingency/Net Funds Flow	30.00
Total	**$1,705.20**

Source: The Atlanta Committee for the Olympic Games. 1997. The Official Report of the Centennial Games. Atlanta: Peachtree Press.

TABLE 4

CODA Public Spaces Projects				
Project	Local public sources	Federal funds	Private and foundation funds	Total cost
Peachtree Street Corridor/Hardy Ivy Park	$6,098	$6,500	$1,077	$13,675
Auburn Avenue Corridor	$3,169	$2,600	$100	$5,869
Auburn Market/ Dobbs Plaza	$1,948	$1,200	$74	$3,222
Atlanta University Center/Westside Corridor	$4,867	$3,140	$3,619	$11,626
Capitol Avenue Corridor	$1,840	$4,000	$270	$6,110
International Blvd Corridor/Walton Spring Park	$4,703	$3,200	$459	$8,362
Ralph David Abernathy Corridor and Square	$1,813	$2,130	$265	$4,208
Georgia Avenue Corridor	$63	$1,230	$70	$1,363
Tenth Street Corridor	$27	$0	$965	$992
Woodruff Park	$48	$0	$5,887	$5,935
Marietta Corridor and Parks	$2	$0	$150	$152
Ga. Tech-Freedom Park Bikeway	$75	$240	$40	$355
Freedom Park	$50	$0	$730	$780
Founders' Park/ Summerhill Street Extensions	$325	$510	$29	$864

CODA Public Spaces Projects				
Project	Local public sources	Federal funds	Private and foundation funds	Total cost
Local Neighborhood Streets	$7,167	$0	$0	$7,167
Design, Development, Other Projects, Contingency	$493		$3,785	$4,278
Total	**$32,688**	**$24,750**	**$17,520**	**$74,958**

Sources: Atlanta Neighborhood Development Partnerships, Corporation for Olympic Development in Atlanta, Housing Resource Center, Federal Reserve Bank Neighborhood Community Development Corporation, Amy Zeller

TABLE 5

Investments in CODA Redevelopment Neighborhoods by 1997 (millions of dollars)				
Neighborhood	Est. Total Pre-Olympic Investment	Est. Private Pre-Olympic Investment	Est. Public Pre-Olympic Investment	Approx. Private/ Public Ratio to Date
Butler/Auburn	$32,004	$7,462	$24,542	1:3
Old Fourth Ward	$4,927	$1,696	$3,231	1:2
Mechanicsville	$11,661	$3,367	$8,294	1:2.5
Peoplestown	$8,703	$2,442	$6,261	1:2.5
Summerhill	$30,485	$14,897	$15,588	1:1
Total	**$87,780**	**$29,864**	**$57,916**	

Source: R. Beagle. CODA memorandum. February 1996

TABLE 6

Federal Funding Provided to the 1996 Olympic Games (1999 dollars in thousands)			
Federal Department or Agency	ACOG planning and staging the games	CODA/ City preparing the host city	Major components and other notes
Department of Agriculture	19,530	2,059	Whitewater venue and various landscaping
Department of Commerce	4,337	4,966	EDA infrastructure / RDA Boulevard
Department of Defense	36,339	2,434	Safety and security services
Department of Education	7,419	7,304	Admin and staff / Paralympics
Department of Energy	4,686	-	Swimming venue solar water heating
Department of Health and Human Services	5,110	-	Public health, security services
Social Security Administration	1,565	-	Paralympic ceremonies
Department of Housing and Urban Development	2,087	15,643	Public housing renovation, community planning services
Department of the Interior	1,562	13,019	MLK District development, safety and security
Department of Justice	22,449	-	Security and staffing; FBI, DEA, Immigration, ADA, US Marshals
Department of Labor	3,036	-	Paralympic volunteers

Federal Funding Provided to the 1996 Olympic Games (1999 dollars in thousands)			
Federal Department or Agency	ACOG planning and staging the games	CODA/ City preparing the host city	Major components and other notes
Department of State	1,044	-	Increased agency services
Department of Transportation: FHA, FTA, FAA, FRA	22,781	369,370	Road and bridge projects, signage, Intelligent transportation services, mass transit projects, Olympic Transportation security
Department of the Treasury	7,082	-	Safety and security services, IRS, Customs, Secret Service, BATF
Department of Veterans Affairs	1,716	-	Safety and security services
Corporation for National and Community Services	3,130	-	Safety and security services
EPA	8,210	-	Safety and security services, infrastructure
FCC	39	-	Communications systems improvement
FEMA	11,602	-	Safety and security services
Federal Executive Board	1,821	-	Safety and security services
GSA	2,086	-	Paralympics admin and staffing
TVA	5,118	-	Whitewater venue construction
USIA	7,551	-	Information Programs

Federal Funding Provided to the 1996 Olympic Games (1999 dollars in thousands)			
Federal Department or Agency	ACOG planning and staging the games	CODA/ City preparing the host city	Major components and other notes
USPS	4,293	16,428	Increased postal services
Total	184,593	423,910	Total federal expenditure: $608,503,000

Source: U.S. General Accounting Office. 2006. Olympic Games; Federal Government Provides Significant Funding and Support. Report to Congressional Requesters. General Accounting office. September.

TABLE 7

Significant Supporting Investments to the 1996 Olympics (Permanent investment by 1996, millions of dollars)			
Source	Included in federal funds, Table 6	Separate funding	Total
MARTA (transit)	114.0	n.a.	114.0
GDOT (highways)	214.8	n.a.	214.8
Hartsfield Airport		600.0	600.0
Georgia Power		67.0	67.0
Total	328.75	667.0	996

Sources: Federal Funds Table 4-5; Atlanta Hartsfield Jackson website; Georgia Power interview with Kay B Lee.

TABLE 9

Key Economic Benefits and Costs of the Games		
	Benefits	**Costs**
Pre-Games Phase	Tourism Construction activity	Investment expenditures Preparatory operational costs Lost benefits from displaced projects
Games Phase	Tourism Stadium & Infrastructure Olympic Jobs Revenues from the Games Tickets, TV rights, sponsorship	Operational expenditures Congestion Lost benefits from displaced projects
Post-Games Phase; the Legacy	Tourism Stadiums and Infrastructure Human Capital Urban regeneration International reputation	Maintenance of venues and infrastructure Lost benefits from displaced projects

Source: Holger Pruess, 2004: Economist Intelligence Unit; Legacy 2012: understanding the impact of the Olympic Games

TABLE 10

Cost per Ticket Sold; Olympic Host Cities from 1988 to 2012

Host City	Total Cost ($ billion)	Tickets Sold ($ million)	Cost per Ticket (dollars per ticket sold)	$0	$1,000	$2,000	$3,000	$4,000	$5,000	$6,000
1988 Seoul	4.0	3.3	$1,212							
1992 Barcelona	9.3	3.0	3,100							
1996 Atlanta	3.0	8.5	352							
2000 Sydney	5.6	6.7	985							
2004 Athens	9.0	3.8	2,370							
2008 Beijing	44.0	6.5	6,142							
2012 London	14.6	8.2	1,780							

Source: compiled by authors.

Table 11

Financial Balance of Olympic Games Organizing Committees
($US millions, 1995 prices)

	Operational costs	Revenues	Balance excluding investments	Overall balance
Munich '72	546	1,090	544	-687
Montreal '76	399	936	537	-1,228
Los Angeles '84	467	1,123	656	335
Seoul '88	512	1,319	807	556
Barcelona '92	1,611	1,850	239	3
Atlanta '96	1,202	1,686	484	0
Sydney 2000	1,700	1,900	239	0

Source: Preuss, 2004: Economist Intelligence Unit; Legacy 2012: understanding the impact of the Olympic Games

Table 12

Costs and Impact of Past Summer Olympic Games, 1988–2012

Host city	Initial budget estimate	Final estimated total costs	Economic impact	Period
Seoul, 1988	US$2.0 B	n.a.	US$ 300 M	1982–1988
Barcelona, 1992	n.a.	n.a.	0.03	1987–1992
Atlanta, 1996	n.a.	US$2.6 B	US$ 5.1 B	1991–1997
Sydney, 2000	A$1.9 B	US$4.9 B	6.5	1994–2006
Athens, 2004	US$6.1 B	US$12.5 B	US$15 B	
Beijing, 2008	US$2.0 B	US$46.0 B	US$ 146 M	
London, 2012	US$3.8 B	US$12.9 B		

Source: Preuss, 2004: Economist Intelligence Unit; Legacy 2012: understanding the impact of the Olympic Games

Table 13

Public Sector Costs and Revenues for the 1996 Olympics (millions of dollars in year 1996)			
Government level	Costs	Tax revenue	Total
Local	148.1	24.0	(124.1)
State	153.2	176.4	23.2
Federal	367.0	182.7	(184.3)
Total	$668.3	$383.1	($285.2)

Source: Larry Keating, Atlanta Race, Class, and Urban Expansion, 2001

DIFFERENT STUDIES SHOW DIFFERENT values in nearly all these categories. Wherever possible we have used the values from the IOC fact sheet of 2014 Source: Economist Intelligence Unit; Legacy 2012: Understanding the Impact of the Olympic Games

BIBLIOGRAPHY

Andraovich, Greg, Michael J. Burbank and Charles H. Heying. "Olympic Cities: Lessons Learned from Mega-Event Politics." *Journal of Urban Affairs* 23, no. 2 (2001).

Atlanta Committee for the Olympic Games. *Community Outreach, ACOG's Legacy of Human Impact.* Atlanta: ACOG, 1997.

———. *The Cultural Olympiad.* Atlanta: ACOG, 1997.

———. *The Official Report of the Centennial Games. Atlanta: Volume I, Planning and Organizing; Volume II, The Centennial Olympic Games; Volume III, The Competition Results.* Atlanta: Peachtree Press, 1997.

Bayor, Ronald H. *Race and the Shaping of Twentieth-Century Atlanta.* Chapel Hill: University of North Carolina Press, 2001.

Beatty, Anita. *Atlanta's Olympic Legacy.* Geneva: Centre on Housing Rights and Evictions, 2007.

Bertaud, Alain, and Harry W. Richardson. "Transit and Density: Atlanta, the United States and Western Europe." University of Washington. http://courses.washington.edu/gmforum/Readings/Bertaud.pdf.

Blackmon, Douglas A. *Slavery by Another Name: The Re-Enslavement of Black Americans from the Civil War to World War II.* New York: Anchor Books, 2009.

Bullard, Robert D. *The Black Metropolis in the Twenty-First Century: Race, Power, and the Politics of Place.* Lanham, MD: Rowman & Littlefield, 2007.

Bullard, Robert D., Glenn S. Johnson and Angel O. Torres. *Sprawl City: Race, Politics, and Planning in Atlanta.* Washington, D.C.: Island Press, 2000.

Corporation for Olympic Development in Atlanta (CODA). *The CODA Master Development Plan*. 1993.

Dobbins, Michael. "Race and Class in Atlanta-Style Development." In Etienne and Faga, *Planning Atlanta*.

Dobbins, Michael, Leon Eplan and H. Randal Roark. "Atlanta's Olympic Legacy." In *Mega-Event Cities: Urban Legacies of Global Sports Events*, edited by Valerie Viehoff and Gavin Poynter. London: Routledge, 2018.

———. "The Centennial Olympics, Atlanta, Georgia, USA, 1996." Paper at the Olympic Legacy Conference, University of East London, London, 2013.

Economist Intelligence Unit. "Legacy 2012: Understanding the Impact of the Olympic Games." *Economist*, 2012.

Engle, Sam Marie. "The Olympic Legacy in Atlanta." *University of New South Wales Law Journal* 22, no. 3 (1999): 902–8.

Eplan, Leon S. "The Genesis of Citizen Participation in Atlanta." In Etienne and Faga, *Planning Atlanta*.

Etienne, Harley F., and Barbara Faga, eds. *Planning Atlanta*. Chicago: American Planning Association, Planners Press, 2014.

French, S.P., and M.E. Disher. "Atlanta and the Olympics: A One Year Retrospective." *Journal of the American Planning Association* 63, no. 3 (1997): 379–92.

Frey, William H. *Population Growth in Metro America since 1980: Putting the Volatile 2000s in Perspective*. Brookings Metropolitan Program, March 2012. https://www.brookings.edu/research/population-growth-in-metro-america-since-1980-putting-the-volatile-2000s-in-perspective.

Gravel, Ryan. *Where We Want to Live: Reclaiming Infrastructure for a New Generation of Cities*. New York: St. Martin's Press, 2016.

Hobson, Maurice J. *The Legend of the Black Mecca: Politics and Class in the Making of Modern Atlanta*. Chapel Hill: University of North Carolina Press, 2017.

Keating, Larry. *Atlanta: Race, Class, and Urban Expansion*. Philadelphia: Temple University Press, 2001.

Keating, Larry, Max Creighton and Jon Abercrombie. "Community Development: Building on a New Foundation." In Sjoquist, *Olympic Legacy*.

Lomax, Michael L. "The Arts; Atlanta's Missing Legacy." In Sjoquist, *Olympic Legacy*.

Newman, H.K. "Neighborhood Impacts of Atlanta's Olympic Games." *Community Development Journal* 34, no. 2 (1999): 151–59.

Olympic Games: Federal Government Provides Significant Funding and Support. Report to Congressional Requesters. Washington, D.C.: U.S. General Accounting Office, 2006.

Padgett, Richard W., and James R. Oxendine. "Economic Development: Seeking Common Ground." In Sjoquist, *Olympic Legacy*.

Patton, Carl V. "Downtown: The Heart and Soul of Atlanta." In Sjoquist, *Olympic Legacy*.

Pendergrast, Mark. *City on the Verge: Atlanta and the Fight for America's Urban Future.* New York: Basic Books, 2017.

Piper, Valerie. *Case Study Atlanta.* Washington, D.C.: Brookings Institution, 2005.

Pomerantz, Gary M. *Where Peachtree Meets Sweet Auburn: The Saga of Two Families and the Making of Atlanta.* New York: Penguin Books, 1996.

Preuss, Holger. *Economic Dimension of the Olympic Games.* Barcelona: Centre d'Estudis Olympics (UAB), 2002.

Quesenberry, P. "The Disposable Olympics Meets the City of Hype." *Southern Changes* 18, no. 2 (1996): 3–14.

Roark, Randal. "Atlanta; Formal Paradoxes and Political Paratactics." In *Atlanta*, edited by Jordi Bernado and Ramon Prat. Barcelona: Actar, 1995.

———. "The Legacy of the Centennial Olympic Games." In Etienne and Faga, *Planning Atlanta*.

Roark, Randal et al. *The Civic Trust.* Atlanta: The Corporation for Olympic Development in Atlanta, 1995.

Rutheiser, Charles. *Imagineering Atlanta. The Politics of Place in the City of Dreams.* London: Verso, 1996.

Sjoquist, David L. et al. *The Olympic Legacy: Building on What Was Achieved.* Atlanta: School of Policy Studies, Georgia State University, 1996.

Stone, Clarence N. *Regime Politics: Governing Atlanta.* Lawrence: University of Kansas Press, 1989.

Wolfe, Thomas. *Man in Full.* New York: Farrar, Straus and Giroux, 1998.

ACKNOWLEDGEMENTS

For such a lengthy and complex story, there is a cast of hundreds, each playing important roles across the span of the Olympic period. Many we have acknowledged in the text, others here, yet surely some will be left out, and for that we apologize. We do, however, want to especially recognize the invaluable contribution of three individuals who have advised us since the beginning of the project in 2011 and who themselves played pivotal roles in the success of the city's Olympic period.

Clara Axam, a daughter of Atlanta's civil rights generation and a longtime public servant, supported the improvement of Atlanta's civic life through roles including Director of Administrative Services for the City of Atlanta and Deputy Superintendent of Atlanta Public Schools in charge of a massive upgrade of school facilities. She was the President of the Corporation for Olympic Development in Atlanta (CODA), the entity at the center of this story and a great resource and reviewer of our work. Without her skills as a master facilitator of communication and consensus building among disparate interests, we might not even have a story to tell.

Charlie Battle, an Atlanta attorney, lifelong Olympics enthusiast and consultant on other Olympics bids, member of the original bid committee for the Olympics, was an officer of the Atlanta Committee for the Olympic Games (ACOG).

David Sjoquist was the chief of research for Research Atlanta, an arm of Georgia State University, and a core staff member to the Atlanta Renaissance Board, whose city summary he edited. Subsequently, he edited

The Olympic Legacy: Building on What Was Achieved report, which provided important information and insights to the authors.

We would like to extend a special thanks to those directly involved in our project—Joe Gartrell, the acquisitions editor at The History Press, without whom this would not have become a book; Abigail Fleming, History Press editor, patiently helping us to make the book readable; Jeb Dobbins, the photographer for the legacy projects and one of the book's cover images, whose insightful photography sharpened our message; Kelsey Keane, our patient grammar editor early on, and we surely needed that; and Megan Barrow, who provided editorial guidance as we struggled along in the early days.

For the genesis of this book, we must credit Margarita Sanudo, a Swiss city planning student who was undertaking a doctoral dissertation in 2010 at ETH Zurich. She was studying four Olympic cities: Barcelona, Atlanta, Sydney and Athens. Unlike the other three, she noted a paucity of information about Atlanta, with no complete or consistent account. She showed up in Atlanta one afternoon in 2011, looking for someone who might fill her in on these issues. She contacted Mike Dobbins seeking information about the Atlanta Games, and he brought in the other two of us. That contact, along with reviewing what she had been finding, prompted us to undertake this book, including doing our own research on the other three cities for comparison purposes. And we are indebted to Tom Weyandt, Director of the City's Bureau of Planning, and later Executive Director of Research Atlanta Inc. for his early advice on the book.

Following Mayor Andrew Young, whose role was pivotal in winning the Games, Mayors Maynard Jackson Jr. and Bill Campbell were at the helm of city government for almost the entire span covered in the book, and without their support during that time, again, we may not have had anything to write about. Mayor Jackson's COO, John Reid, provided useful insights in framing this book. Among Mayor Campbell's top administrative staff and cabinet members, Byron Marshall, Steve Labovitz, Sharon Gay, Susan Pease Langford, Greg Pridgeon, Doug Hooker, later Larry Wallace and many others excelled in working through the often thorny mazes of city hall to deliver what had to be delivered. Mayor Shirley Franklin, who succeeded Bill Campbell, extended the period when city planning and design mattered and brought invaluable experience from her extensive city hall past and in her Olympics role as ACOG's community liaison officer.

As referenced in the book, we would also like to thank again the team of young planners, architects and landscape architects who, as project managers for CODA, provided the dedication and energy to actually make the CODA projects become reality in time for the Games: Stan Harvey, Bob Begle, Danita Brown, John Threadgill, Patricia Kerlin and Ginny Kennedy. As the CODA crew disbanded, we must add plaudits for the City Planning Department's urban design section with its chief Alycen Whiddon along with Aaron Fortner, Caleb Racicot and Enrique Bascunana, along with guidance from Fernando Costa, Beverly Dockery-Ojo and Renee Kemp Rotan. This talented and hardworking bunch provided the continuity to carry many CODA initiatives forward while generating many new initiatives following the Games. All of these professionals, young at the time, have gone on to productive and civic-minded careers and together constitute another dimension of the legacy of the Games.

The hardworking staff members of city, partnering agencies, county, state and federal government, some of whom noted in the book but too often unsung, deserve credit for doing their parts to step up with the common purpose of implementing the Games and the follow-up successfully. Likewise, community and neighborhood leaders, many mentioned in the book, played important roles in guiding the Olympic efforts toward better outcomes for their communities in the years that followed, roles that some are still performing.

The CODA photo archives used extensively in the book are large with many contributors, but we have relied heavily on the work of professional photographers Dixi Carrillo, Beatriz Coll, Neil Dent and Drew Logothetis.

And the authors especially credit their spouses and families for boosting their efforts along the way, while suffering the downsides of lost time and attention associated with three old guys trying to recap their histories.

ABOUT THE AUTHORS

LEON S. EPLAN, FAICP, was twice Atlanta's commissioner of planning and development before and then during the six-year lead-up to the Games. He previously served as professor and director of the Graduate Program of City Planning at Georgia Tech. He initiated and prepared the City's Olympic Development Program (ODP) and then helped to establish its Corporation for Olympic Development in Atlanta, the body assigned to implement the ODP. Active throughout his long practice of planning in local and national planning organizations, Eplan was twice elected as national president of the American Institute of Planning, the forerunner of today's American Institute of Certified Planners. He is a fellow in that organization. For many years, he was president of Eric Hill Associates, then one of the largest private consulting firms in the South.

RANDAL ROARK, FAICP, is a retired professor of the College of Design at the Georgia Institute of Technology. His private practice in planning and architecture over the past fifty years has included both public and private projects across the country. He has also worked as a consultant for the Department of the Interior, as consulting director of the Blueprints for Successful Communities Initiative of the Georgia Conservancy and as the first chairman of the Atlanta Urban Design Commission. He served as director of planning and design for the Corporation for Olympic Development in Atlanta for the design of public projects in preparation for the 1996 Centennial Olympic Games. He has received numerous awards, among which are professor emeritus and distinguished professor at Georgia Tech, Conservationist of the Year in Georgia from the Georgia Conservancy, an AICP Best Comprehensive Plan for Small or Rural Communities for the Covington 2050 Plan and the Atlanta AIA Ivan Allen Award for Professional Public Service. He currently lives in St Augustine, Florida, with his wife, Ann, of fifty-two years.

MICHAEL DOBBINS, FAICP, FAIA, is professor of practice in Georgia Tech's College of Design, teaching urban design and studio courses in the School of City and Regional Planning. He succeeded Eplan in 1996, becoming Atlanta's commissioner of planning, development and neighborhood conservation for the following six years. Serving in that position during and after the Games, he was able to finalize several uncompleted ODP projects following the Games, as well as oversee several major post-Olympics initiatives that were related to or induced by the Games.

Visit us at
www.historypress.com